W9-ADB-073

Leaves

of

Grass

America's Lyric-Epic
of Self and Democracy

TWAYNE'S MASTERWORK STUDIES

Robert Lecker, General Editor

Leaves

of

Grass

*America's Lyric-Epic
of Self and Democracy*

JAMES E. MILLER, Jr.

TWAYNE PUBLISHERS • NEW YORK
Maxwell Macmillan Canada • Toronto
Maxwell Macmillan International • New York   Oxford
Singapore   Sydney

Twayne's Masterwork Studies No. 92

Leaves of Grass: America's Lyric-Epic of Self and Democracy
James E. Miller, Jr.

Twayne Publishers
Macmillan Publishing Company
866 Third Avenue
New York, New York 10022

Maxwell Macmillan Canada, Inc.
1200 Eglinton Avenue East
Suite 200
Don Mills, Ontario M3C 3N1

Macmillan Publishing Company is part of the Maxwell Communication Group
of Companies.

Library of Congress Cataloging-in-Publication Data
Miller, James Edwin, 1920–
    Leaves of grass : America's lyric-epic of self & democracy / James E.
Miller, Jr.
      p.   cm. — (Twayne's masterwork studies ; no. 92)
    Includes bibliographical references and index.
    ISBN 0-8057-8089-0—ISBN 0-8057-8565-5 (pbk.)
    1. Whitman, Walt, 1819–1892. Leaves of grass. 2. Epic poetry,
American—History and criticism. 3. Democracy in literature.
4. Self in literature. I. Title. II. Series.
PS3238.M53 1992
811'.3—dc20   92-1188
                                              CIP

The paper used in this publication meets the minimum requirements of American
National Standard for Information Sciences—Permanence of Paper for Printed
Library Materials. ANSI Z3948-1984. ∞ ™

10 9 8 7 6 5 4 3 2 1 (hc)
10 9 8 7 6 5 4 3 2 1 (pb)

Printed in the United States of America

Not I, not any one else can travel that road for you,
You must travel it for yourself.

W.W.

The clock indicates the moment—but what does
eternity indicate?
W.W.

CONTENTS

This picture of Whitman appeared in the 1855 edition of *Leaves of Grass*, replacing the author's name; readers were able to find Whitman's name only by reading the initial long poem, later called "Song of Myself," where he included it in a line: "Walt Whitman, a kosmos, of Manhattan the son." He indicated that he considered the picture as an integral part of his book, and he included it in some later editions of *Leaves*. It is a steel engraving of a daguerreotype.

NOTE ON THE REFERENCES
AND ACKNOWLEDGMENTS

All quotations from *Leaves of Grass* are identified in the text by poem title and, when applicable, section number; thus readers may find the quotations easily in any available edition of *Leaves*. For my source, I have used my edition of Whitman, *Complete Poetry and Selected Prose* (Boston: Houghton Mifflin Co., 1959), which is based on the 1891–92 "Authorized Edition" (with corrections as indicated by recent textual scholarship). I have also used my edition as source for the Whitman prose pieces contained in it: the 1855 Preface, the 1872 Preface to *As a Strong Bird on Pinions Free*, the 1876 Preface to *Two Rivulets*, the 1888 Afterword, "A Backward Glance O'er Travel'd Roads," and *Democratic Vistas*. All quotations from these prose works are cited in the text by page numbers in parentheses. Quotations from other Whitman works and other authors and editors are fully cited in the notes.

I have drawn on a large body of criticism and scholarship read over a period of many decades. The Selected Bibliography at the end contains many items and I am indebted to virtually all of them in one way or another. I must, however, mention in passing the work of Gay Wilson Allen, particularly his biography (*The Solitary Singer*, 1955,

1967, 1985) and handbooks (*Walt Whitman Handbook*, 1946; *The New Walt Whitman Handbook*, 1975, updated 1986; and *A Reader's Guide to Walt Whitman*, 1970), and the work of Ed Folsom and William White in editing the ongoing *Walt Whitman Quarterly*, which contains a current and exhaustive bibliography in each issue.

Though I have benefited from the work of many others, my view of Whitman is my own, developed over the last half century. I found, indeed, that in formulating my "reading" of *Leaves of Grass* for this book I was consciously and unconsciously drawing on my own past work. This includes not only the books of mine listed in the bibliography, but also numerous scattered essays on Whitman published from 1955 on, and including especially "Walt Whitman's Omnisexual Vision" (in *The Chief Glory of Every People*, ed. Mathew J. Bruccoli, 1973) and "Whitman's *Leaves* and the American 'Lyric Epic' " (in *Poems in Their Place*, ed. Neil Fraistat, 1986). Although my perspective on Whitman has remained generally consistent, it has not remained unchanged. I like to think that in subtle ways it has deepened and broadened. Certainly my enthusiasm for reading him and my regard for his art and substance have never waned.

CHRONOLOGY:
WALT WHITMAN'S LIFE, WORKS, AND TIMES

1819	Walt Whitman born 31 May, in rural West Hills, Long Island, the second child in a rapidly growing family. His quick-tempered father struggles to eke out a living on a farm as his cheerful, self-possessed mother devotes herself to bearing nine children and caring for her family.
1823	The family moves to Brooklyn, where Whitman's father works as a carpenter.
1825–1830	Attends public school in Brooklyn.
1830	Works as office boy for a lawyer and a doctor.
1830–1835	Learns and works at printing trade.
1836–1838	Teaches at various schools in Long Island.
1838–1839	Edits the *Long Islander*, a weekly newspaper.
1840–1841	Campaigns for reelection of Democrat Martin Van Buren, who loses; teaches school; works as a printer in New York City.
1842	Edits New York newspapers and publishes *Franklin Evans; or, The Inebriate: A Tale of the Times*, a temperance novel.
1843–1845	Edits or contributes to various newspapers and magazines.
1846–1847	Edits the Brooklyn *Daily Eagle*.
1848	Quits or is forced to resign from the *Daily Eagle* in January because of activities in the Free-Soil party, which opposes the extension of slavery into territories obtained in the war with Mexico. Supports Martin Van Buren as presidential candidate

for the Free-Soil party. From February to May, travels with his brother Jeff to New Orleans, going by rail and stagecoach to and over the Allegheny mountains, then by steamboat on the Ohio and Mississippi rivers. Works in New Orleans on the *Crescent* and returns to New York via the Mississippi and the Great Lakes.

1848–1849   Edits the Brooklyn *Freeman*, a Free-Soil paper.

1850–1854   Runs a stationery store and printing business; works as a carpenter and house builder.

1855   Publishes by himself, probably on 4 July, the first edition of *Leaves of Grass* containing a preface and twelve poems, each entitled "Leaves of Grass." Distributes copies to well-known writers and receives Emerson's letter of congratulations dated 21 July.

1856   Publishes the second edition of *Leaves of Grass* containing 32 poems bearing individual titles and, at the end, Emerson's letter together with a long reply; on the spine of the book he quotes, without authorization, from Emerson's letter: "I greet you at the beginning of a great career." Is visited by Bronson Alcott and Henry David Thoreau.

1857   Is visited by Ralph Waldo Emerson.

1857–1859   Edits Brooklyn *Daily Times*; frequents German bohemian restaurant, Pfaff's, in New York.

1860   Goes to Boston to oversee publication of the third edition of *Leaves of Grass*, the first by a commercial publisher. The book contains 124 new poems, many of them in titled clusters; the arrangement of the poems reflects an embryonic structure suggestive of Whitman's epic intent. In a stroll on Boston Common, Whitman rejects Emerson's advice to exclude "Children of Adam" and other sex poems.

1861   As the Civil War begins Whitman's Boston publisher fails, but the third edition continues to circulate through unauthorized use of the plates.

1862   Goes to Civil War battlefield in Virginia to find his wounded brother, George; finds his brother recovering but many comrades maimed and suffering, needing help.

1863–1865   Becomes the "wound-dresser," visiting and tending the sick and injured in Washington; develops intimate friendship with horse-car conductor, Peter Doyle.

1865   Begins working in the Indian Bureau of the Department of Interior. Publishes *Drum-Taps*, to which he adds "When Lilacs

Chronology: Walt Whitman's Life, Works, and Times

Last in the Dooryard Bloom'd" and other poems as an annex after Lincoln's assassination in April. Is removed from his job in June because his sex poems are considered indecent, but is immediately appointed to a position in the Attorney General's office.

1866   W. D. O'Connor publishes *The Good Gray Poet*, defending Whitman from charges of obscenity.

1867   John Burroughs publishes *Notes on Walt Whitman as Poet and Person*. Whitman publishes the fourth edition of *Leaves of Grass*, revealing his intent to shape the whole of his poetry, including the Civil War and Lincoln poems, into a single structure which follows roughly the contours of his life and times, opening with an announcement of themes in the book's initial poem, "Inscription" ("One's Self I Sing") and concluding with an intimate farewell to the reader in the poem-cluster, "Songs Before Parting."

1868   William Michael Rossetti publishes in England a selection of *Leaves* entitled *Poems of Walt Whitman*, omitting poems treating sexual themes.

1869   Mrs. Anne Gilchrist, widow of the William Blake biographer Alexander Gilchrist, reads Rossetti's edition of Whitman's poems, falls in love with him, and writes "An Englishwoman's Estimate of Walt Whitman" (published in the Boston *Radical Review* in 1870).

1871–1872   Whitman publishes the fifth edition of *Leaves of Grass* and *Democratic Vistas*, dated 1871; publishes the *Passage to India* pamphlet, which is then included without change of pagination in a reissue of the fifth edition with the date 1872; like the fourth edition, the fifth shows Whitman's continuing determination to fashion a structure for his *Leaves* that will include the whole body of his poetry and the entire range of his and his country's experiences as he imaginatively or mythically conceives them.

1873   Suffers a paralytic stroke; his mother dies; Whitman moves from Washington, D.C., to Camden, New Jersey.

1875   Publishes *Memoranda During the War*.

1876   Publishes "Centennial Edition" of *Leaves* in two volumes, one a reissue of the 1871 *Leaves* and the other entitled *Two Rivulets*. About this time begins rest and recuperation visits to the Stafford Farm on Timber Creek. English admirer Anne Gilchrist arrives in Philadelphia and begins long friendship with Whitman.

1879–1880   Whitman travels West to the Rockies; visits the alienist Dr. R. M. Bucke in Canada.

1881–1882   Publishes the sixth edition of *Leaves* in Boston. Although new poems will be added later, the book now assumes a structure containing poems in versions and positions that will remain fixed in the final publication of the work. The book is banned in Boston because the Society for the Suppression of Vice finds it immoral; Whitman transfers its publication to Philadelphia.

1882   Publishes *Specimen Days & Collect*, an autobiographical reminiscence and narrative fragments, including *Memoranda During the War*.

1883   Dr. R. M. Bucke publishes *Walt Whitman*, a biography on which Whitman has collaborated.

1884   Whitman buys house on Mickle Street, Camden, New Jersey, where he remains until his death.

1888   His paralysis increases. Publishes *November Boughs*, including the poem-cluster "November Boughs" and the prose piece "A Backward Glance O'er Travel'd Roads." Horace Traubel makes the first of his many visits with the poet, keeping a detailed record to be published later in the multi-volumed *With Walt Whitman in Camden*.

1889   Whitman publishes a volume combining the 1881 edition of *Leaves* with the 1882 *Specimen Days* and the 1888 *November Boughs*.

1891   Publishes *Good-Bye My Fancy* containing a cluster of poems and miscellaneous prose pieces.

1892   Issues the "authorized" *Leaves of Grass*, sometimes called the "deathbed edition"; the text incorporates the sixth edition (1881–82) bound together with the poem-clusters (called Annexes) "Sands at Seventy" from *November Boughs* and "Good-Bye My Fancy," and concludes with the prose piece "A Backward Glance O'er Travel'd Roads." Whitman selects the title "Old Age Echoes" for a final cluster of poems that will be added as a third Annex in an issue of this edition in 1897. Dies 26 March and is buried in a tomb prepared in Harleigh Cemetery, Camden, New Jersey.

Literary and Historical Context

1

The Prolonged Birth Pangs of the Nation

In 1819, the year Walt Whitman was born, the United States of America had been in existence for only some thirty years. The seemingly significant dates in American history were: the Revolutionary War to gain independence from the "mother country," England, 1775–83; the Declaration of Independence, 4 July 1776; the Constitutional Convention called to formulate a federal constitution for the victorious thirteen colonies, 1787; the formal approval of the Constitution by each of the colonies, 1787–90.

Those who participated in these events were aware that the significance of what they were doing in creating the first democracy in the modern world was to have resonance far beyond America's shores and far beyond the eighteenth century. There were poets of the time who realized that the deeds of valor and the acts of statesmanship cried out for imaginative embodiment in story and song. In short, the epic deeds needed an epic poet. Philip Freneau (1752–1832), who lived through and wrote about the stirring events of the times in his lyric poems, became known as the "poet of the American Revolution." Joel Barlow (1754–1812), who attempted to embody the actions of the era in the traditional epic genre, produced *The Columbiad* in 1807 (a reworking of his *The Vision of Columbus*, 1787), but its stilted heroic couplets and pretentious visionary structure conspired against its success. Neither Freneau nor Barlow was able to work the apparently heroic materials into enduring epic form. Other writers less talented tried and failed.

Was there something amiss with the times or the poets? Was there something left unfinished in the founding, something that would require even greater heroic deeds and more creative acts of statesmanship? The 1776 Declaration of Independence had proclaimed: "We hold these truths to be self-evident, that all men are created equal, that they are endowed by their Creator with certain unalienable Rights, that among these are Life, Liberty and the pursuit of Happiness."[1] This apparently all-inclusive sentence in reality excluded from its sweep the entire population of slaves, then numbering about 500,000 individuals. If the Declaration had been adopted as Thomas Jefferson, himself a Virginia slave-holder, had originally written it—identifying slaves not as property but as human beings—it would have abolished slavery. But the Southern states refused to sign without deletion of this provision.

Another missed opportunity came with the Constitutional Convention in 1787. When the Convention decided that the number of representatives from each state would be determined by population, the question arose as to how to count the slaves. Northerners argued that since the slaves were property, they should not be counted; Southerners now argued that slaves were individuals and therefore should be counted. A compromise was reached providing for the counting of three-fifths of the slave population for each state—in effect designating a slave as equal to three-fifths of a person. Another compromise was reached on the question of the slave trade by postponing action on its prohibition for 20 years, until 1808. The possibility of giving the vote to women, who were universally disenfranchised, was not even considered.

It is obvious that the compromises made in the process of drawing up the founding documents creating the United States of America undermined—radically and fundamentally—the creation of a genuine democracy, leaving the political structure deeply flawed, and postponing until an indefinite time in an uncertain future the ultimate fate of the fledgling nation. By the time of the appearance on the scene of Walt Whitman—who would come to style himself the "poet of democracy" as well as the "poet of America"—national politics had come to be characterized by controversies and conflicts between proslavery and antislavery individuals and parties over the slavery question. The woman suffrage movement, though not in the forefront of political debate, also had its beginnings during this period.[2]

From the time of Whitman's birth until 1860, when Whitman reached his forty-first year, the slavery issue had simmered and simmered but did not come to a furious boil until the outbreak of the Civil War that year. There were a number of compromises that repeatedly postponed the day of reckoning. The first of these was the Missouri Compromise of 1820, which admitted Missouri as a slave state and Maine as a free state (thereby maintaining an even balance between slave and free states), and barred slavery from the territory of the Louisiana Purchase lying north of 36° 30' and west to the Rocky Mountains.

There was continuing confrontation in Congress on the issue, with the block of slave states and the block of free states constantly maneuvering against each other to gain the upper hand. After much controversy, Texas was annexed as a slave state in 1845. The advent of the War with Mexico (1846–48) brought the Wilmot Proviso (passed by the House but never approved by the Senate) barring slavery from territories gained in the war. The Compromise of 1850 admitted California as a free state, but left New Mexico and Utah to settle the matter for themselves; it abolished the slave trade in Washington, D. C., but provided more stringent laws for dealing with fugitive slaves. The Kansas-Nebraska Act of 1854 provided for popular (or "squatter") sovereignty on the question of slavery in these two states.

The 1857 Dred Scott decision of the U. S. Supreme Court, finding that runaway slaves had no legal rights (they were "property," not U. S. citizens), took the issue out of the hands of Congress and repealed the Missouri Compromise. The South seemed to have won the legal battle over slavery by judicial decree. The remnants of the Free-Soil party, formed in 1847–48 to oppose the extension of slavery, had joined with others of similar views in 1854 to form the Republican party, and in 1860 it selected Abraham Lincoln, an obscure lawyer from Illinois, as its candidate. Pledging opposition to the extension of slavery, Lincoln won the election in November and soon after the Southern slave states began to secede from the Union.

As a journalist as well as a poet during this period, Whitman was keenly aware of the issues and even became involved in the disputes. He had joined the breakaway democrats to support the candidacy of Martin Van Buren on the Free-Soil party ticket in the presidential election of 1848. Van Buren was defeated, and Whitman lost his job as editor of the Brooklyn *Daily Eagle* (probably because of his Free-Soil sympathies). When the Southern states began to secede and form the Confederacy in 1860–61, in effect forming two Americas, the "poet of America" was by definition on the side of the Union. The war began in April 1861, not long after the inauguration of Abraham Lincoln, who had pledged to preserve the Union. Preserve it he did, and he also issued the Emancipation Proclamation in 1863—the first step in the freeing of the slaves that was fully achieved with the adoption in 1865 (after Lincoln's assassination in April) of the thirteenth amendment to the Constitution abolishing slavery and involuntary servitude.

By the time of the Civil War, Whitman had published the first three editions of *Leaves of Grass*. But many of his most moving poems were written about the war and his role in it as a "Wound-Dresser," published in 1865 as *Drum-Taps*. Even more moving were the poems Whitman wrote about Abraham Lincoln after the president's assassination (including the great elegy "When Lilacs Last in the Dooryard Bloom'd"), published also in 1865 as *Sequel to Drum-Taps* (the title became "Memories of President Lincoln" in the 1881 edition of *Leaves*).

These poems were later integrated into his masterwork, *Leaves of Grass*, as Whitman came to realize the importance of the Civil War and its consequences for America and for himself in his assumed role as poet of America. Heretofore Whitman had been ambitious to become the "poet of democracy" and thus the "poet of America." The war appeared to have brought to completion something left unfinished in the years of the country's founding. Whitman put the idea this way in "A Backward Glance O'er Travel'd Roads" (1888): "I went down to the war fields in Virginia (end of 1862,) lived thenceforward in camp—saw great battles and the days and nights afterward—partook of all the fluctuations, gloom, despair, hopes again arous'd . . . along and filling those agonistic and lurid following years, 1863–'64–'65— the real parturition years (more than 1776–'83) of this henceforth homogeneous Union. Without those three or four years and the experiences they gave, *Leaves of Grass* would not now be existing" (450).[3]

Although the Civil War was the "real parturition"—or birth—of America in that it guaranteed the endurance of the Union and abolished slavery, the period after the war did not bring to flower the democratic ideal Whitman envisioned for the country. Indeed, corruption was rampant in many departments of government while many ruthless individuals in business and industry became "robber barons," geniuses at cornering or manipulating markets, accumulating great wealth through unscrupulous exploitation of others, including underpaid and unprotected workers. As for the former slaves, most found their lot in the impoverished South little changed socially or economically. In his prose pamphlet *Democratic Vistas*, published in 1871, Whitman acknowledged and cataloged many of the country's shortcomings and called for a spiritual force to counter the materialistic forces gaining dominance in America. The democratic ideal, he believed, was by no means a reality in the present, but endured only in poetic, or spiritual, "vistas"—visionary glimpses into future possibilities.

When Whitman died in 1892, the American frontier extending west to the Pacific had been officially declared settled. The number of states in the Union had doubled from 22 in 1819 (the year of Whitman's birth) to 44 in 1890. All of the land that would make up the 48 contiguous states had come under federal control. The population had grown from some 10 million in 1820 to over 60 million in the 1890s. The largely agricultural country of Whitman's birth, made up of farms, small towns, and vacant land, was rapidly becoming a country of factories, cities, and suburbs. The Spanish-American War, waged shortly after Whitman's death (1898), revealed a new international role for America as a world power, taking over from Spain in Cuba and in the Philippine Islands an imperialistic presence.

In living through the key nineteenth-century decades that shaped America and embodying that experience in his masterpiece *Leaves of Grass*, Whitman staked out his claim as America's epic poet and as the poet of democracy. Although at times he found himself beset by doubts about the direction or destiny of America and the democratic tenets proclaimed at its founding and sealed in blood at its "parturition" in the Civil War, he never wavered in his fundamental commitment to the democratic ideals he envisioned in the "vistas" he imaginatively embodied in his poetry and prose.

2

A New Poetry for the New Nation

Leaves of Grass commands attention because of its uniquely poetic embodiment of America's democratic ideals as written in the "founding" documents of both the Revolutionary War and the Civil War and in the blood spilled by the soldiers of both wars. The credentials supporting its claims to be America's epic are impressive and worthy of consideration even by those who might take exception to such claims. Moreover, its form—the free-verse lyric epic—invented and developed by Whitman to contain his personal, national, and world vision, has had an incalculable influence on successor poets both in America and throughout the world—an influence that has continued into the twentieth century. Those who feel indifference (or hostility) to Whitman's substance must still come to recognize the vitality and durability of his poetic techniques and strategies, and the frequent employment of them by some of the very poets who have condemned him most sharply.

Near the end of "Song of Myself," in Section 51, Whitman says: "Do I contradict myself? / Very well then I contradict myself, / (I am large, I contain multitudes.)" Whitman's confession of inconsistency is made out of his realization that his work embodies seemingly

9

opposing views: his idea of democracy holds in tension both individuality and "En-Masse"; his notion of the self embraces both physicality and spirituality; his identity as an American includes both national and international dimensions; his conception of poetic form stretches to include both free verse and structured poetry; his reinvention of the heroic tribal (or national) poem incorporates both the private confession and the public chant, the lyric voice and the epic vision.

In the first poem of *Leaves of Grass*, "One's-Self I Sing," readers encounter immediately the core of the work's democratic vision: "One's self I sing, a simple separate person, / Yet utter the word Democratic, the word En-Masse." The opening line of the book defines the self in its essence as *detached* ("separate"); the word "Yet" at the beginning of the second line swerves the meaning away from detachment to *attachment* ("En-Masse"); the two lines together proclaim the crosscurrents of the theme that was in effect the original and basic inspiration for launching the *Leaves*. The theme achieved its most magnificent embodiment in two early poems: "Song of Myself," which stands today, a century and a half after it was written, as one of the greatest expressions of identity and individuality ever to be penned; and "Crossing Brooklyn Ferry," which remains one of the most passionate and compelling affirmations of the generational interrelatedness, unity, and solidarity of aggregate humanity ever conceived.

Whitman recognized the complexities and challenges of this seemingly simple central theme of his *Leaves*. In remembering the origins of his masterpiece in "A Backward Glance O'er Travel'd Roads," Whitman asks: "Of the great poems receiv'd from abroad and from the ages, and to-day enveloping and penetrating America, is there one that is consistent with these United States, or essentially applicable to them as they are and are to be? Is there one whose underlying basis is not a denial and insult to democracy?" (448). The question is rhetorical and Whitman asks it primarily to point to his fundamental intention in embarking on his epic enterprise. Although Whitman encapsulates his central purpose in simple terms, he realizes its ambiguities and difficulties: "Democracy has been so retarded and jeopardized by powerful personalities, that its first instincts are fain to clip, conform, bring in stragglers, and reduce everything to a dead level. While the ambitious thought of my song is to help the forming of a great aggregate Nation, it is, perhaps, altogether through the forming of myriads of fully develop'd and enclosing individuals" (451).

In elaborating his theme of individuality in "Song of Myself," Whitman again confronts a paradox—the self's divided nature, embodying both the physical and the spiritual: "I believe in you my soul, the other I am must not abase itself to you, / And you must not be abased to the other." These lines in Section 5 of "Song of Myself" lead into a scene of mystical union, with the soul holding the body in a kind of sexual thrall, the interpenetration and interfusion suggesting the inseparability of the self's two dimensions. The remainder of "Song of Myself" moves back and forth in profound exploration of the dual yet mystically unified nature of being.

In celebrating the physical dimension of the self, Whitman openly and joyously celebrates sexuality, violating many of the sexual taboos of the day and thereby earning himself the opprobrium of many readers, including the influential writer who had begun by lavishly praising the *Leaves*, Ralph Waldo Emerson. Whitman recognized both the centrality and the diversity of the sexual dimension of the self, and attempted to do it justice poetically in the companion clusters of poems, "Children of Adam" and "Calamus." Whereas "Song of Myself" focuses in part on the autoerotic awakening of the individual, the two following clusters focus, in turn and in part, on the heteroerotic (male-female relationships) and the homoerotic (same-sex relationships).

But the sexuality of the *Leaves* is by no means confined to a few lines or a handful of poems. When Whitman reviewed his poetic achievement in "A Backward Glance," he wrote:

> "*Leaves of Grass* is avowedly the song of Sex and Amativeness, and even Animality—though meanings that do not usually go along with those words are behind all, and will duly emerge; and all are

sought to be lifted into a different light and atmosphere. Of this feature, intentionally palpable in a few lines, I shall only say the espousing principle of those lines so gives breath of life to my whole scheme that the bulk of the pieces might as well have been left unwritten were those lines omitted. . . . The vitality of it is altogether in its relations, bearings, significance—like the clef of a symphony. At last analogy the lines I allude to, and the spirit in which they are spoken, permeate all of *Leaves of Grass*, and the work must stand or fall with them, as the human body and soul must remain as an entirety." (452)

No other poet, before or after Whitman, has so insisted on the theme of sexuality (or "Animality"), or handled it so subtly, delicately, and deeply, or diffused it so comprehensively as he has done throughout the whole of his work. Perhaps the secret of Whitman's success was his intuitive understanding of the transcendent relationship and inseparability of the physical and the spiritual, the sexual and the mystical.

Whitman was as innovative in his form as he was in his subject matter. He was the first American poet to see that, as America had begun a heretofore untried experiment in democratic governance, so the American poet must find a new epic form to match. His invention was what can only be described as the "lyric-epic," a term embodying a paradox to equal all the paradoxes embodied in the substance of *Leaves*. The work is a single poem made up of a medley of shifting voices—lyric and bardic, youthful and mature, assertive and groping. The songs and chants are shaped into a coherent work, with beginning, middle, and end, following the contours of the poet's life as he lived it through the momentous and formative events of America's nineteenth century. But the poetic form of the songs and chants—free verse—is as revolutionary as the new structure Whitman invented: like the fledgling democracy they celebrated, the form and structure broke from tradition and started boldly up new paths, untried roads. These paths and roads are still under exploration by those Whitman addressed in an "Inscriptions" poem, "Poets to Come":

I myself but write one or two indicative words for the future,
I but advance a moment only to wheel and hurry back in the darkness.

A New Poetry for the New Nation

I am a man who, sauntering along without fully stopping, turns a casual
   look upon you and then averts his face,
Leaving it to you to prove and define it,
Expecting the main things from you.

3

The Fight of a Book for the World

Whitman himself undertook the job not only of printing the 1,000 copies of the first edition of *Leaves of Grass* in 1855 but also that of distributing the book. He sent out gift copies to established poets of the day. John Greenleaf Whittier was said to have been offended by the frankness of the poetry and to have thrown his copy into the fire. Fortunately for Whitman, Ralph Waldo Emerson—the reigning man of letters in America at the time—retained his copy and was so impressed by the book of the unknown poet that he immediately wrote a letter to Whitman (dated 21 July). It read, in part: "I am not blind to the worth of the wonderful gift of *Leaves of Grass*. I find it the most extraordinary piece of wit and wisdom that America has yet contributed. I am very happy in reading it, as great power makes us happy. . . . I give you joy of your free and brave thought. . . . I find incomparable things said incomparably well, as they must be. I find the courage of treatment which so delight us, and which large perception only can inspire."[1]

Emerson's extravagant praise, together with the sparsity of reviews of the book, may have emboldened Whitman to write a number of unsigned reviews himself, one of which began: "An American bard at last! One of the roughs, large, proud, affectionate, eating, drinking, and breeding, his costume manly and free, his face sunburnt and bearded, his postures strong and erect, his voice bringing hope and prophecy to the generous races of young and old."[2] Whitman's self-laudatory reviews did not in essence claim more than Emerson in his note had affirmed for *Leaves of Grass*, and Whitman was fully aware of the possible public value of such a personal letter.

In preparing a second edition of his work for publication in 1856, Whitman decided to exploit Emerson's letter to the full. He did not ask Emerson's permission probably because he feared he would be refused. The 1856 edition carried on the spine of the book a quotation from the Emerson letter: "I Greet You at the/ Beginning of A / Great Career / R. W. Emerson." Few people walking into a bookstore that carried Whitman's new edition could fail to be impressed by such an extraordinary endorsement from such an eminent man of letters. And if they picked up the book and turned to the end, they found the whole of Emerson's letter together with a long reply from Whitman. The reply opened: "Dear Master: Here are thirty-two Poems, which I send you, dear Friend and Master, not having found how I could satisfy myself with sending any usual acknowledgment of your letter."[3] In effect, Whitman trapped the sage of Concord by going public with the correspondence. It seems likely that Emerson would indeed have refused a request for permission to publish his letter, given the recommendation he made later, when the third edition of the *Leaves* was in preparation for publication in Boston, that Whitman delete from his book all the lines and poems referring to sex. Although Emerson never attempted to withdraw his first glowing approval of Whitman's *Leaves*, neither did he ever again publicly comment on the book. There is no doubt, however, that Emerson's letter opened doors for Whitman's *Leaves* that would otherwise have remained shut.

Although good luck seemed to attend the issuance of the first two editions of Whitman's *Leaves*, both privately printed, the third edition issued in Boston in 1860 had the bad luck of appearing on the eve of the Civil War and finding its publisher, Thayer and Eldridge, soon in bankruptcy. The plates for the book, however, were acquired by an unscrupulous publisher, who sold pirated copies. Although the surreptitious publisher acted unethically and Whitman went without royalties, *Leaves of Grass* continued to be circulated, and to develop a special, if not a wide, readership.

It would be gratifying to report that within a few years of its publication *Leaves of Grass* had achieved the worldwide reputation it now enjoys in the late twentieth century. Such was not the case. The story of its recognition as a poetic masterpiece is a story of fits and starts or advances and retreats. One of the books written on the reception of the *Leaves*, by William Sloane Kennedy, is appropriately entitled *The Fight of a Book for the World* (1926). The account of this "fight" up to 1892, the year of Whitman's death, shows that Whitman himself figured prominently in developing the strategy for the various skirmishes. After 1892, it was left to a band of friends and admirers, who knew both Whitman and his book, to carry on the battle until it was gradually taken over by those who knew the man only through the book. Ultimately, of course, it was *Leaves of Grass* itself that brought to the "fight" the seeds of victory and triumph, persuading readers of its own true worth.

The first book (or pamphlet) to be published on Whitman appeared in 1866, and was written by the poet's personal friend W. D. O'Connor. He entitled his work *The Good Gray Poet* because it was primarily a defense of Whitman after he was fired from his government clerkship by James Harlan, Secretary of the Interior, for being the author of a book "full of indecent passages" (Whitman had taken his manuscript to the office, where he began revising it during spare moments for the fourth edition, 1867; Harlan came upon it there). O'Connor, a fellow government clerk, wrote his work primarily as a vindication of Whitman, but his characterization of *Leaves* was perceptive: "At most, our best books were but struggling beams; behold in *Leaves of Grass* the immense and absolute sunrise! It is all our own! The nation is in it! In form a series of chants, in substance it is an epic of America. It is distinctively and utterly American. Without model, without imitation, without reminiscence, it is evolved entirely from our own polity and popular life."[4] In his 1868 short story, "The Carpenter,"[5] O'Connor presented a Christ-like portrait of Whitman.

John Burroughs, another of Whitman's friends (and later to achieve fame as a nature essayist), in 1867 published the first biography of Whitman, *Notes on Walt Whitman as Poet and Person*, including in it an analytical interpretation of his poetry.[6] Whitman cooperated with Burroughs in the writing of the book, especially in the biographical section, and initiated or acceded to many of the myths that later biographers would discover to be either distortions or inventions. In 1868, the British critic and poet William Michael Rossetti edited *Poems by Walt Whitman* for publication in Great Britain. By publishing a selection instead of the complete fourth edition, Rossetti was able to set aside the poems he believed to be "gross" or "crude"— words he used in his introductory essay to characterize some of Whitman's poetic flaws.[7]

As Whitman's poems became known in Great Britain, he attracted a number of distinguished British admirers, including Mrs. Anne Gilchrist, widow of Alexander Gilchrist, the biographer of William Blake. Her essay, "An Englishwoman's Estimate of Walt Whitman," appeared in a Boston journal in 1870 and pointed out for special praise Whitman's frankness in dealing with sexuality in his poetry.[8] Later (1876), she moved her family to Philadelphia to be near the poet, hoping to find a mate but finding instead a warm friend. The British poet Algernon Swinburne published his highly appreciative long poem "To Walt Whitman in America" in his *Songs Before Sunrise*, 1871. It opens:

> Send but a song oversea for us,
>   Heart of their hearts who are free,
> Heart of their singer, to be for us
>   More than our singing can be.[9]

After Swinburne became acquainted with the whole body of Whitman's poetry, including those poems too "gross" or "crude" to be included in the British edition, he changed his mind about the "good gray poet" and revised his opinion in public in an 1887 essay.[10] The British classical scholar with a special interest in Greek friendship, John Addington Symonds, read Whitman's poetry as a young man and was indelibly impressed. He later began a correspondence with Whitman, described in his *Walt Whitman: A Study* (1893), pressing him on the meaning of the cluster of friendship poems in *Leaves of Grass* entitled "Calamus"; Whitman's evasive reply, quoted by Symonds, referred to his "jolly" "times South" and to six illegitimate children (all pure fabrication according to later biographers).[11]

Although Whitman could exert little control over his image abroad as his fame spread, he could still shape that image in America. The Canadian alienist (or psychiatrist) Dr. R. M. Bucke, whom Whitman met on a trip through Canada in 1877, became a close friend of the poet and began collecting material for a biography, published in 1883. It was entitled simply *Walt Whitman*,[12] and was written in part by Whitman himself. As in his collaboration with John Burroughs earlier, Whitman was able to inject biographical material more in harmony with the bardic Whitman projected in *Leaves of Grass* than with the factual Walter Whitman of bones and blood. It was Bucke who developed the concept of rare individuals gifted with superior or transcendent awareness, a concept he described in full in his book *Cosmic Consciousness*, published in 1901; he cited Whitman (alongside Gautama the Buddha and Jesus the Christ) as one of his prime examples.[13]

Whitman had not by the time of his death in 1892 achieved the popularity in America he had hoped for when he began writing the poems for *Leaves of Grass* some forty-five years before. Ralph Waldo Emerson was more respected and Henry Wadsworth Longfellow more beloved. But Whitman's reputation at home was solid enough to attract curious readers and critics in the future. And his budding influence abroad was to increase remarkably so as to surprise many of the poet's countrymen who had disdained to read him. By the centennial year of Whitman's death—1992—it could be affirmed that Whitman was viewed world-wide as America's preeminent poet whose democratic themes embodied an urgency important to all humankind and whose free verse style and lyric-epic form provided models on which poets of the future might build.

The two leading American poets of the modernist movement begun in the early twentieth century, Ezra Pound and T. S. Eliot, clearly had feelings of antipathy toward Whitman, but felt that they could not ignore him. It is a tribute to Whitman's vitality and durability that he was the only predecessor American poet whom Pound and Eliot felt it necessary to disavow; by their very disavowal they revealed the depth of their uneasiness about *Leaves of Grass* as a threat to their own work. Pound's views about Whitman are found in two remarkable pieces: a brief essay called "What I Feel About Walt Whitman" (1909), whose tone is a strange blend of grudging respect, envy, and rage; and the short poem "A Pact," in which Whitman is addressed as a "pig-headed father."[14] Eliot was even more dismissive of Whitman than was Pound, revealing in one essay[15] that he "had to conquer an aversion to his form, as well as to much of his matter" in order to read him, and referring in an aside to the "large part of clap-trap in Whitman's content."

But Whitman had his defenders during the modernist period, including the poets Edgar Lee Masters, Carl Sandburg, William Carlos Williams, Hart Crane, and Langston Hughes as well as the biographers and critics Bliss Perry, Emory Holloway, and Henry Seidel Canby. It was not, however, until the latter half of the twentieth century that Whitman came into his own in America. The centennial year of the first edition of *Leaves of Grass*, 1955, may be conveniently taken as the turnaround year, marking the appearance of Gay Wilson Allen's biography, *A Solitary Singer*, and Richard Chase's critical work, *Walt Whitman Reconsidered*. Such literary movements as that of the Beat Generation, in which Whitman figured as a kind of patron saint, issued "founding" documents that were clearly marked by his influence: Allen Ginsberg's *Howl*, 1956, and Jack Kerouac's *On the Road*, 1957. By the last decade of the twentieth century, there was a plethora of American books about Whitman, proving among other things that he did indeed "contain multitudes." And there seemed a plethora of poets bent on writing the great American long poem in some variation of the free verse form and the lyric-epic structure that Whitman had pioneered in *Leaves of Grass*.

Paralleling this general acceptance of Whitman at home was the

establishment of him abroad as the preeminent American poet. In
Europe, and especially in Great Britain, France, and Germany, Whitman has had a following since the nineteenth century. During the
period of the cold war (1945–90), there developed an appreciation of
Whitman in the iron curtain countries, especially Russia, because he
was understood as a "socialist" poet. In China, 1991 saw the publication of the first complete translation into Chinese of *Leaves of Grass*.
In Japan and India, it has been Whitman's mystical side that has
made him appreciated, imaginatively transfigured into an intuitive Zen
Buddhist or expounder of the *Bhagavad-Gita*. And there has been no
warmer reception of Whitman than that granted by writers of the
Latin American countries, who have discovered in Whitman the ways
of being a "New World poet." Two of the most distinguished Latin
American writers (one who received the Nobel Prize and the other
who should have received it) have paid homage to Whitman in their
poetry and prose: the Chilean poet Pablo Neruda and the Argentinean
fabulist Jorge Luis Borges.[16]

Would Whitman have been surprised at his standing as a world
poet one hundred years after his death? Probably not, if we are to
judge by his anticipation of such a position by many hints in *Leaves
of Grass*, including the brief "Inscriptions" poem entitled "To Foreign
Lands":

I heard that you ask'd for something to prove this puzzle the New World,
And to define America, her athletic Democracy,
Therefore I send you my poems that you behold in them what you
    wanted.

A Reading

4

The Lyric-Epic Structure

It is best at the beginning to make a quick journey through the whole of *Leaves of Grass* to see what kind of structure we have encountered. Just as we give the once-over to a building we have entered to comprehend the nature of its architecture and its arrangement of space, so should we observe the structure of the *Leaves*, to see how the parts fit into and interconnect with the whole.

Many lyric poets, as they near the end of their careers, choose to arrange their poems in the chronological order in which they were written, thus giving the reader a sense of their development and growth. Whitman deliberately chose not to follow this traditional method. Instead, he spent a lifetime shaping and reshaping *Leaves of Grass* through six editions and several reissues (reprintings of an edition often bound with groups of separately paginated new poems at the end) to find the form of the book he wanted finally to leave the world. He placed an author's note at the beginning of the 1891–92 "deathbed edition" (really a reissue of the 1881 sixth edition with the addition of new clusters of poems entitled "Annexes"): "As there are now several editions of L. of G., different texts and dates, I wish to say that I prefer and recommend this present one, complete, for future printing, if there should be any; a copy and fac-simile, indeed, of the text of these 438 pages. The subsequent adjusting interval which is so important to form'd and launch'd work, books especially, has pass'd; and waiting till fully after that, I have given (pages 423–438) my concluding words. W. W." (1).

The important word here for those beginning a journey through *Leaves* is *form'd*. Whitman is clearly concerned in this passage that posterity encounter the book as he has put it together—formed it—in this final version. And just as he launched the work in 1855 with a preface describing his plans for the future, so in this 1891–92 version he has appended (pp. 423–38) "A Backward Glance O'er Travel'd Roads" reviewing, assessing, and speculating on his achievement. It is in this prose afterword that we may find the clues as to the nature of the form into which Whitman—at least as he saw it—has in the end cast his masterpiece.

Throughout "A Backward Glance," Whitman relates the origins of his poem to the nature and development of America: "Behind all else that can be said, I consider *Leaves of Grass* and its theory experimental—as, in the deepest sense, I consider our American republic itself to be, with its theory" (444). Why not, he considers, rely on the great poems of the past from abroad, before which he has stood "with uncover'd head, fully aware of their colossal grandeur and beauty of form and spirit" (448–49). He then encapsulates his sense of the inadequacies of the epics of the past together with his vision of America's radically new meaning that requires a new poetic voice: "As America fully and fairly construed is the legitimate result and evolutionary outcome of the past, so I would dare to claim for my verse. Without stopping to qualify the averment, the Old World has had the poems of myths, fictions, feudalism, conquest, caste, dynastic wars, and splendid exceptional characters and affairs, which have been great; but the New World needs the poems of realities and science and of the democratic average and basic equality, which shall be greater" (449).

Those national poems before which Whitman had stood with bared head were epics: long narrative poems written in an exalted style, with a central character of station and stature performing heroic deeds of discovering, founding, or conquering, in wars and on battlefields where the fate of a people or a country hung in the balance. Conceived in such a tradition, the American epic might cast as its hero Christopher Columbus or George Washington; indeed, forerunners of Whitman, including Timothy Dwight in *The Conquest of Canaan* (1785) and Joel Barlow in *The Columbiad* (1787, 1807) had tried to write just such epics. It was Whitman's genius to realize, intuitively, that as America was different from countries of the past, so its epic might have another kind of hero compatible with that difference. He says in "A Backward Glance" that in his early thirties he began to feel the emergence of an inchoate inspiration: "This was a feeling or ambition to articulate and faithfully express in literary or poetic form, and uncompromisingly, my own physical, emotional, moral, intellectual, and aesthetic Personality, in the midst of, and tallying, the momentous spirit and facts of its immediate days, and of current America—and to exploit that Personality, identified with place and date, in a far more candid and comprehensive sense than any hitherto poem or book" (444).

Here is the germ of Whitman's radical innovation. His inspiration is lyric, his ambition epic, the one to be fitted within the structure of the other. A lyric is traditionally defined as a short poem expressing the thoughts and feelings of the poet or speaker. On the surface, the lyric appears poles apart from the epic, embodying as it does the poet's own "physical, emotional, moral, intellectual, and aesthetic Personality." But Whitman in effect decided to cast himself in the role of his own epic hero, using his lyric gift not only to express himself but also to "tally" the "momentous spirit and facts" of his "immediate days, and of current America." His eyes would be turned both inward and outward, and his voice would be both personal and public. His qualifications for appearing as the hero of America's epic were those very qualities disdained by past epics: he was one of the average, with a station neither above nor below that of others, identifying with "the working-man and working-woman," and ready to "endow the democratic averages of America" with the "ranges of heroism and loftiness" that the "Greek and feudal poets" reserved for their "lordly born characters" (452).

We know certainly from "A Backward Glance" that Whitman's

intention was epic, and his form as he gradually conceived it was best defined as "lyric-epic." The opening cluster of poems in the *Leaves* is entitled "Inscriptions," suggestive of those carved writings we often find on entering community or public buildings; the last clusters are entitled "Annexes," suggestive of the additions to buildings made after the basic structures have been completed. As we linger before the edifice reading the various inscriptions we find there in an arranged order, we discover a series of announcements of what is to come after we enter: there is first, in the tradition of the epic, an announcement of themes together with a reference to a muse:

One's-self I sing, a simple separate person,
Yet utter the word Democratic, the word En-Masse.

Of physiology from top to toe I sing,
Not physiognomy alone nor brain alone is worthy for the Muse, I say the
    Form complete is worthier far,
The Female equally with the Male I sing.

Of Life immense in passion, pulse, and power,
Cheerful, for freest action form'd under the laws divine,
The Modern Man I sing.

This poem announces the major themes to be dramatized in the epic it opens, themes that differentiate it from the epics of the past. The poet opens, in the first two lines, with an announcement of his political themes (freedom and equality, identity and fraternity); moves in the next three lines to themes of individuality (soul and body, intellectuality and sexuality, feminine and masculine); and concludes in the last lines focusing on themes of life (passion and power, vitality and potentiality, freedom and discipline). Lurking in every corner of the poem are contradiction and paradox. And at the beginning as well as at the end stands ambiguously revealed the hero of this strange epic, "simple," not special, "separate," yet of the "En-Masse," not above it: "Modern Man." Not "Myself I sing" but "One's-self I sing" (the linguistic formulation remains singular but includes the reader) opens the poem and book. With "One's-self" Whitman launches that act of merging his "self" with the "self" of the reader, a merging into "Oneness" ultimately to be consummated in the *Leaves*. In the closing line of the poem, both poet and reader are caught up in the identity marking their crucial differentiation from the heroes of past epics—"Modern Man."

This differentiation is elaborated in the second "Inscriptions" poem, "As I Ponder'd in Silence," by metaphoric linkage with past epics. As the poet sits brooding over his poems, a threatening "Phantom" appears—"The genius of poets of old lands"—and, pointing to the "immortal songs" of the past, chides the poet for not realizing that they all had "but one theme": *the theme of War, the fortune of battles./ The making of perfect soldiers.* To this muse of past epics (*"haughty Shade"*) the poet answers that he, too, indeed sings war, but it is in his book *"with varying fortune, with flight, advance and retreat, victory deferr'd and wavering."* The field of battle is the world, and hanging in the balance in this metaphoric battle is fulfillment of all the vital themes embodied in the book: *"For life and death, for the Body and for the eternal Soul./ Lo, I too am come, chanting the chant of battles,/ I above all promote brave soldiers."*

Having launched his epic in "Inscriptions" and defended to the haughty muse its distinctive differences from epics of the past, the poet begins his journey with the reader—that important "You" who is a constant presence throughout the *Leaves* and whom the poet addresses with passionate tone at critical junctures on the shared journey. The incorporation of the reader as a principal character, accompanying and identifying with the poet in his role of epic hero, may have been Whitman's most stunning innovation. None of his followers to the present day has been able to pull off such a brilliant poetic trick. At the end of "Inscriptions" the poet says in a two-line poem: "Thou reader throbbest life and pride and love the same as I, / Therefore for thee the following chants."

Following the dedicatory poems of "Inscriptions" comes the programmatic and mythically biographical "Starting from Paumanok" (Paumanok is the Indian name for Long Island, where Whitman was born), which offers a kind of outline of the book that is to follow, a mélange of its thoughts and feelings, a medley of its recurrent themes. As "Starting from Paumanok" progresses, the poet turns more and more, as in Section 9, to the technique of direct address—talking intimately to You:

> What do you seek so pensive and silent?
> What do you need camerado?
> Dear son do you think it is love?
> Listen dear son—listen America, daughter or son,
> It is a painful thing to love a man or woman to
>   excess, and yet it satisfies, it is great.

"Starting from Paumanok" is a poem mapping a journey, the emblematic journey enacted in the whole of *Leaves of Grass*: an archetypal journey of life.

The last lines of "Starting from Paumanok," lines of great emotional intensity, are addressed passionately to the reader:

O camerado close! O you and me at last, and us two only,
O a word to clear one's path ahead endlessly!
O something ecstatic and undemonstrable! O music wild!
O now I triumph—and you shall also;
O hand in hand—O wholesome pleasure—O one more desirer and lover!
O to haste firm holding—to haste, haste on with me.

No longer are You, the reader, outside the book, observing the poet on his journey. You are there inside the book, by the poet's side—just the two of you ("us two only"), filling the role of the poet's "camerado," holding his hand ("hand in hand"), and becoming his "desirer and lover." The ecstatic fervency of the passage is unmistakable. The whole poem has been surging to this final direct appeal, and it serves not only as a conclusion to "Starting from Paumanok" but also as the beginning of the central body and substance of *Leaves of Grass*.

Let us turn next to the end of the book, setting aside those clusters of poems that Whitman clearly meant as ancillary to the main structure of *Leaves of Grass* when he labelled them "Annexes." The book's true conclusion is the cluster of poems entitled "Songs of Parting," ending with the remarkable poem "So Long!" The closing section of "So Long!" contains perhaps Whitman's most fervently intimate lines addressed to the reader in the whole of *Leaves of Grass*:

> Camerado, this is no book,
> Who touches this touches a man,
> (Is it night? are we here together alone?)
> It is I you hold and who holds you,
> I spring from the pages into your arms—decease calls me forth.
>
> Oh how your fingers drowse me,
> Your breath falls around me like dew, your pulse lulls the tympans of
>   my ears,
> I feel immerged from head to foot,
> Delicious, enough.

The sexual overtones of the passage are so unmistakable as to make many readers uncomfortable. But the moment of the poet's immediate presence passes and he makes ready his departure:

> Dear friend whoever you are take this kiss,
> I give it especially to you, do not forget me,
> I feel like one who has done work for the day to retire awhile,
> I receive now again of my many translations, from my avataras ascending,
>   while others doubtless await me,
> An unknown sphere more real than I dream'd, more direct, darts
>   awakening rays about me, *So long*!
> Remember my words, I may again return,
> I love you, I depart from materials,
> I am as one disembodied, triumphant, dead.

The language conjures up a lovebed/deathbed scene, in which the reader becomes the spouse or lover as the beloved bids a final farewell. Some readers are repelled by such intimacy, feeling as though their privacy has been invaded. And it has been, of course. Whitman's intent throughout *Leaves of Grass* is to invade the privacy of his reader, stripping away all that conceals the real self underneath.

As we turn from the opening and close of *Leaves of Grass* to glance at the book's main body, we find the reader lurking everywhere, particularly in those key transitional passages in individual poems as well as in the structural groupings of poems. Before proceeding to define the structure of Whitman's book, however, we should step back and take a look at the three phases that may be detected in the growth of Whitman's masterpiece. As each of these phases drew to a close and a new one began, Whitman thought he was launched on a new book— yet always ended up integrating the poems of the new phase into *Leaves of Grass*.

In Phase One, 1855–60, encompassing the first three editions of *Leaves of Grass* (1855, '56, '60), "Song of Myself" is, thematically, the foundation poem.

In Phase Two, 1860–71, encompassing the fourth (1867) and fifth (1871) editions, the Civil War and Lincoln poems are planned and appear as a separate volume (*Drum-Taps*, 1865), but Whitman changes his mind and integrates the poems in the fifth edition of *Leaves*.

In Phase Three, 1871–81, encompassing the two-volume Centennial or "Author's Edition" of 1876 and the sixth edition, 1881, the "Passage to India" poems are planned as independent of the *Leaves*, but are ultimately integrated in the 1881 edition, the edition in which Whitman created the basic structure of his book that would remain intact in the future.

Keeping these three phases in mind, we may gain insight into the differentiation among the three basic or substantive parts in the body of the *Leaves* by examining various comments Whitman made about his intentions as his plans were evolving and shifting. First, it may be best to look again at one of the last of Whitman's comments on his work, "A Backward Glance," particularly at his emphatic remarks on the importance of the role of the Civil War in his book: "Although I had made a start before, only from the occurrence of the Secession War, and what it show'd me as by flashes of lightning, with emotional depths it sounded and arous'd . . .—that only from the strong flare and provocation of that war's sights and scenes the final reasons-for-being of an autochthonic [that is, "original" or "indigenous"] and passionate song definitely came forth" (450).

When the Civil War (1861–65) began, Whitman was 41, too old to be drafted; after going to the Virginia battlefields to find his wounded brother George, Whitman saw firsthand in Washington, D. C., the primitive care given in the makeshift hospitals and took on the role of "wound-dresser." The Civil War years "1863–'64–'65," Whitman emphasized in "A Backward Glance," were America's "real parturition years (more than 1776–'83)." In other words, Whitman believed that America's "real" birth came not with the Declaration of Independence and victory in the War for Independence but with the abolition of slavery resulting from Union victory in the Civil War. Without the Civil War years and "the experiences they gave," Whitman concluded, "*Leaves of Grass* would not now be existing" (450).

Of course Whitman had published the first three editions of *Leaves of Grass* before the Civil War, and the third edition published in 1860, with its opening "Proto-Leaf" and its closing "So Long!" had taken on many of the structural characteristics that would be preserved in the final edition. Whitman's comments in "A Backward Glance" on the impact of the Civil War and his experience in it on his work must, therefore, be taken metaphorically: It was the Civil War that in a sense enabled him to be present at the real birth and founding of America, settling once and for all the issue of legalized slavery and finally fulfilling, at least in potentiality, those resounding sentences in the Declaration of Independence of almost a century before.

Thus it is that Whitman's Civil War poems, "Drum-Taps" and "Memories of President Lincoln" (including that greatest of American elegies written on Lincoln's assassination in 1865, "When Lilacs Last in the Dooryard Bloom'd"), together with the post-Civil War poems written in its aftermath—"By Blue Ontario's Shore" and "Autumn Rivulets"—form the great and solid center of *Leaves of Grass*, giving the book its ballast and cargo. In the mid-1860s, when Whitman was still thinking of making of his Civil War poems a book separate from

Leaves of Grass, he said of the poems as a group: "It delivers my ambition of the task that has haunted me, namely, to express in a poem . . . the pending action of this *Time & Land we swim in*, with all their large conflicting fluctuations of despair & hope, the shiftings, masses, & the whirl & deafening din, (yet over all, as by invisible hand, a definite purport & idea). . . ."[1]

The poems and poem-clusters that lead up to this middle, from "Song of Myself," "Children of Adam," and "Calamus" through "Sea-Drift" and "By the Roadside"—mainly but not entirely the poems published in the first three editions of *Leaves*—delineate for the New World a prototype democratic personality, given the name Walt Whitman, and fleshed out with particular focus on the physical, the body (but by no means excluding the spiritual, the soul). At the same time that he characterized his Civil War poems (in the letter just quoted), he differentiated them from the poems of the *Leaves* as it stood in 1860: "I am satisfied with *Leaves of Grass*, (by far the most of it) as expressing what was intended, namely, to express by sharp-cut self assertion, *One's-Self* & also, or may be still more, to map out, to throw together for American use, a gigantic embryo or skeleton of Personality, fit for the West, for native models" (*Corres.* I:247). It is interesting to note that after he had integrated the Civil War poems into the *Leaves* in 1871, Whitman wrote in an 1872 preface (to *As a Strong Bird on Pinions Free*) that the "impetus" behind *Leaves of Grass* (now including "Drum-Taps" and "Memories of President Lincoln") was to produce an "epic of Democracy" (429), and that the work was "the song of a great composite *Democratic Individual*, male or female" (432).

The poems and poem-clusters following the Civil War poems, from "Proud Music of the Storm" through "Whispers of Heavenly Death"—mainly (but not exclusively) poems of the third and last, or "Passage to India," phase, written in the 1870s and early 1880s—bring to the fore the vague presence heretofore hovering in the background, the body's spiritual counterpart, the soul, in the midst of thoughts about death and immortality. In his 1876 preface to Volume II (*Two Rivulets*) of the Centennial Edition of *Leaves of Grass*, Whitman revealed the relationship as he saw it between the poems of the first two phases of the growth of the *Leaves* and the poems of this last phase (at the time he wrote he planned to publish these poems, clustered around "Passage to India," in a separate volume): "It was originally my intention, after chanting in *Leaves of Grass* the songs of the Body and Existence, to then compose a further, equally needed Volume, based on those convictions of perpetuity and conservation which, enveloping all precedents, make the unseen Soul govern absolutely at last. I meant, while in a sort continuing the theme of my first chants, to shift the slides, and exhibit the problem and paradox of the same ardent and fully appointed Personality entering the sphere of resistless gravitation of Spiritual Law" (434).

After surveying the phases of the evolution of *Leaves of Grass* and Whitman's relevant comments about it in his prefaces, reviews, notes, and afterwords, we might lay out the structure in the following way, differentiating titles of poem-clusters from single poems by leaving them without quotation marks:

Leaves of Grass: Prototype Personality for the New World Democracy
 I. Introduction to Themes and Greetings
    Inscriptions
    "Starting from Paumanok"
 II. Gigantic Embryo or Skeleton of Personality
    "Song of Myself"   ⎫
    Children of Adam   ⎬ the self and others
    Calamus   ⎭
    [Song Section]
       "Salut au Monde!"   ⎫
       "Song of the Open Road"   ⎪
       "Crossing Brooklyn Ferry" ⎪
       "Song of the Answerer"   ⎪
       "Our Old Feuillage"   ⎬ the self and the world (place)
       "A Song of Joys"   ⎪
       "Song of the Broad-Axe"   ⎪
       "Song of the Exposition" ⎭

"Song of the Redwood-Tree"
"A Song for Occupations" } the self and the world (place)
"A Song of the Rolling Earth"

Birds of Passage
"A Broadway Pageant" } the self and history (time)
Sea-Drift
By the Roadside

III. This Time and Land We Swim In
   Drum-Taps
   Memories of President Lincoln   national crisis and rehabilitation
   "By Blue Ontario's Shore"
   Autumn Rivulets

IV. The Resistless Gravitation of Spiritual Law
   "Proud Music of the Storm"
   "Passage to India"
   "Prayer of Columbus"
   "The Sleepers"
   "To Think of Time"
   Whispers of Heavenly Death

V. Review of Themes and Farewell
   "Thou Mother with Thy Equal Brood"
   From Noon to Starry Night
   Songs of Parting

VI. Afterthoughts: the Annexes
   Sands at Seventy
   Good-Bye My Fancy
   Old Age Echoes

We have noted that Whitman early on had decided that he would replace the traditional epic hero with himself in his national poem, but it was himself as prototypical American democrat identifiable with Americans "En-Masse." We have also noted that the reader—the ubiquitous "You" in *Leaves*—becomes a major character in the poem, at times a camerado, at times an alter ego, of the ever-present "I," or speaker of the poem. We see this speaker perform amazing imaginative gymnastics, such as leaping from the pages of his book into the reader's arms in "So Long!" A little-noticed lyric entitled "To You" in the "Birds of Passage" cluster of poems reveals Whitman turning this "You" into his creation itself—his poem:

Whoever you are, now I place my hand upon you, that you be my poem,
I whisper with my lips close to your ear,
I have loved many women and men, but I love none better than you.

O I have been dilatory and dumb,
I should have made my way straight to you long ago,
I should have blabb'd nothing but you, I should have chanted nothing
    but you.

I will leave all and come and make the hymns of you,
None has understood you, but I understand you,
None has done justice to you, you have not done justice to yourself,
None but has found you imperfect, I only find no imperfection in you,
None but would subordinate you, I only am he who will never consent to
    subordinate you,
I only am he who places over you no master, owner, better, God, beyond
    what waits intrinsically in yourself.

It is clear that the poet, in turning "You" into his poem, in desiring to "sing such grandeurs and glories about you," bestows, at least momentarily, the role of epic-hero on the reader. Whitman's creation, inclusion, and dramatization of the reader in his *Leaves* is among the most remarkable of his achievements, frequently providing the book's most intimate and memorable scenes, moments of emotional surge, moments of sudden insight, moments of deep awareness, moments of ecstatic bliss. Such a powerful portrayal of the reader derived from a strategy that was a part of Whitman's intention from the beginning, an intention that persisted through the shaping and reshaping of his structure to achieve its epic form at the end. Trying to imagine *Leaves of Grass* without You the reader as a central character in it is like trying to imagine *Paradise Lost* without Adam or Eve.

5

"Song of Myself": Tapping Primal Energies

"Song of Myself" is the "founding" poem of *Leaves of Grass*, appearing as the lead poem of the work's first edition in 1855, and assuming the key opening position in the basic structure as finally shaped in the 1881 edition. In its scope it touches on or elaborates the major themes of the book, political, sexual, spiritual. Whitman often referred to his poems as "songs" or "chants," suggesting that they were meant to be heard. Readers might do well, on initial encounter with "Song of Myself," to take these hints and read the poem aloud, declaiming it in the way Whitman imagined, listening to themselves as they chant. An outdoor setting might enhance the performance and deepen the meaning, especially in the presence of grass, a key image of *Leaves* introduced and elaborated in the poem.

After experiencing the whole poem in such a personal performance, the best way to approach its complexities of meaning is to turn next to savoring the poem's individual lines. One of the most astute of the commentaries that played a part in the turnaround of Whitman's reputation from its nadir during the high modernist (or New Critical) period was entitled "Some Lines from Whitman" (1952), by Randall Jarrell: "To show Whitman for what he is one does not need to praise or explain or argue, one needs simply to quote. He himself said, 'I and mine do not convince by arguments, similes, rhymes, / We convince by our presence.' "[1] Jarrell's article convinced a large audience simply by quoting phrase after phrase, line after line, passage after passage: "Agonies are one of my changes of garments"; "I find I incorporate gneiss, coals, long-threaded moss, fruits, grain, esculent roots, / And am stucco'd with quadrupeds and birds all over"; "Unscrew the locks from the doors! Unscrew the doors from their jambs!"

One of the great pleasures in reading "Song of Myself" is for readers to compile their own lists of favorite lines. The supply seems inexhaustible. I have found one of my favorite passages in Section 44, and have settled on it as one of the most powerful statements of individuality in a poem stressing, as one of its numerous themes, the individual as a "simple separate person" throughout. It provides a good base for launching a discussion of the poem:

I am an acme of things accomplish'd, and I an encloser of things to be.

My feet strike an apex of the apices of the stairs,
On every step bunches of ages, and larger bunches between the steps,
All below duly travel'd, and still I mount and mount.

Rise after rise bow the phantoms behind me,
Afar down I see the huge first Nothing, I know I was even there,
I waited unseen and always, and slept through the lethargic mist,
And took my time, and took no hurt from the fetid carbon.

Long I was hugg'd close—long and long.

Immense have been the preparations for me,
Faithful and friendly the arms that have help'd me.

Cycles ferried my cradle, rowing and rowing like cheerful boatmen,
For room to me stars kept aside in their own rings,
They sent influences to look after what was to hold me.

Before I was born out of my mother generations guided me,
My embryo has never been torpid, nothing could overlay it.

For it the nebula cohered to an orb,
The long slow strata piled to rest it on,
Vast vegetables gave it sustenance,
Monstrous sauroids transported it in their mouths and deposited it
    with care.

All forces have been steadily employ'd to complete and delight me,
Now on this spot I stand with my robust soul.

After reading this aloud with the gusto inherent in the lines one is
tempted to say what Randall Jarrell said (Jarrell, 107) after presenting
a particularly vivid set of Whitman's lines: "One hardly knows what
to point at—everything works."

But there are some elements in the lines quoted worth remarking.
There is first the idea of individuality solidly based not on biblical or
religious grounds but on scientific theory—the theory of evolution.
Evolutionary imagery abounds in this passage, and it is used to enhance
the notion of individuality—and this at a time when many would
decry the theory as diminishing or dehumanizing the individual (especially after Charles Darwin brought together persuasive evidence for
the theory in his *Origin of Species*, 1859). There is, moreover, consider-
able wit in the passage that does not undermine but somehow rein-
forces the serious meaning. The poet is climbing those metaphoric
stairs of time in the intuitive assurance that he existed from the beginning, in the "huge first Nothing" (significantly capitalized, inflating its
importance as surely Something), and that he "slept through the lethargic mist" and "took no hurt from the fetid carbon."

Would anyone want to challenge the brilliance of "lethargic" and
"fetid," or the conception of those "cheerful boatmen" ferrying the
poet's cradle through the endless cycles of time? Imagine the universe
carefully concocting its fantastic plans for the advent of Whitman,
cohering a nebula to an "orb"—creating a world!—for his embryo,
piling the strata through the aeons of geologic time on which to rest

it, feeding the tiny embryo with those eerie "vast vegetables," and assigning those "monstrous sauroids"—enormous lizard-like prehistoric animals—to carry it around in their mouths and deposit it in the assigned place with care! The imagery is both extraordinarily witty and at the same time serious in remythologizing what science had demythologized about the creation of human beings. There is a sense in which the poet is absolutely right, about himself and about us: Whatever the nature of the past, we in our individual natures are products of it, and must, therefore, have existed in that huge first Nothing before the creation of the universe or world and must somehow have endured through all those "bunches of ages," however inchoate our state, however miniscule the matter or antimatter we might have been, whatever seemingly hostile environments or grotesque creatures loomed as threats to our survival through time's endless unfolding.

Note that I have generalized from the "I" of this passage to us, the readers, and to all humankind. Has Whitman invited this kind of generalization? "Song of Myself" opens: "I celebrate myself, and sing myself, / And what I assume you shall assume, / For every atom belonging to me as good belongs to you." Here and throughout, the poet includes the reader, by the recurring intimacy of "private" direct address, in his celebration of individuality; the reader becomes a character at one with the poet, a companion on his journey, an equal sharer of his experiences.

But who is this poet? We have a name to bestow on him, revealed in the first line of Section 24: "Walt Whitman, a kosmos, of Manhattan the son." The line appears autobiographical, in that Walter Whitman did indeed come from New York, the Manhattan metropolis. But this Walt Whitman is also "a kosmos," a world or universe! He is— he contains more than—himself. He is in some sense everybody— everyman and everywoman. This expansive view of the speaker's self is best witnessed in the long catalog of Section 15, beginning: "The pure contralto sings in the organ loft, / The carpenter dresses his plank, the tongue of his foreplane whistles its wild ascending lisp, / The married and unmarried children ride home to their Thanksgiving dinner. . . ." The list goes on and on, very much in the manner of a montage in film or the juxtaposing of randomly selected snapshots of all kinds, levels, and breeds of life, and includes the spinning-girl, the lunatic, the quadroon girl, the half-breed, the "woolly-pates" hoeing in the field under the gaze of the "overseer," the squaw, the opium eater, the prostitute, the president, flatboatmen, coon-seekers, and many more. After this colorful, wide-ranging list of Americans engaged in various occupations and activities, Section 15 concludes: "And these tend inward to me, and I tend outward to them, / And such as it is to be of these more or less I am, / And of these one and all I weave the song of myself."

The poet then begins Section 16 with a direct definition of himself as a "kosmos":

> I am of old and young, of the foolish as much as the wise,
> Regardless of others, ever regardful of others,
> Maternal as well as paternal, a child as well as a man,
> Stuff'd with the stuff that is coarse and stuff'd with the stuff that is fine.

There follows another catalog, embracing those who inhabit the whole of America—from the North to the South, from the Atlantic to the Pacific—and concluding with an all-inclusive identity: "Of every hue and caste am I, of every rank and religion, / A farmer, mechanic, artist, gentleman, sailor, quaker, / Prisoner, fancy-man, rowdy, lawyer, physician, priest." In the brief Section 17, the poet drops his cataloging and says of his "thoughts" that had led to his lists of multiple identities: "These are really the thoughts of all men in all ages and lands, they are not original with me, / If they are not yours as much as mine they are nothing, or next to nothing, / If they are not the riddle and the untying of the riddle they are nothing."

These passages (in Sections 15, 16, and 17) are in effect a fulfillment of the theme promised in the second of the first two lines of the opening "Inscriptions" poem: "One's-Self I sing, a simple separate person, / Yet utter the word Democratic, the word En-Masse." The importance of the theme to *Leaves of Grass* as a whole is suggested

by the closing lines of Section 17: "This is the grass that grows wher-
ever the land is and the water is, / This the common air that bathes
the globe." Whitman introduced the grass metaphor in Section 6 in a
number of exploratory but by no means definitive lines, and its surfacing here suggests its political—that is, democratic—dimension. For
Whitman is a political poet in the passages we have examined and
quoted if he is a political poet in any of his poems. Carefully balanced
throughout this founding poem of the *Leaves* is an emphasis on individuality and on commonality, on self and En-Masse, on freedom and
equality: the two critical ingredients of democracy that, in Whitman's
view, hold each other from crippling anarchy on the one hand, and
paralyzing mediocrity on the other.

There is more to be said about this strong political undercurrent
that runs throughout "Song of Myself," surfacing now and again to
make itself felt as an important dimension in the poem. In the longest
section of "Song of Myself," 33, the poet exclaims, "I am the man, I
suffer'd, I was there." Following comes tumbling out a catalog of
vignettes of the despairing, the rejected, the suffering, one of the most
vivid of which is that of the runaway slave:

I am the hounded slave, I wince at the bite of the dogs,
Hell and despair are upon me, crack and again crack the marksmen,
I clutch the rails of the fence, my gore dribs, thinn'd with the ooze of my
    skin,
I fall on the weeds and stones,
The riders spur their unwilling horses, haul close,
Taunt my dizzy ears and beat me violently over the head with whipstocks.

The poet, instead of passively observing, imaginatively assumes the
identities of all victims, exclaiming: "Agonies are one of my changes
of garments."

This identification with the lowly and outcast reaches something
of a climax in Section 37, opening:

You laggards there on guard! look to your arms!
In at the conquer'd doors they crowd! I am possess'd!

Embody all presences outlaw'd or suffering,
See myself in prison shaped like another man,
And feel the dull unintermitted pain.

The poet proceeds to identify with the mutineer, the "youngster . . . taken for larceny," the cholera patient, and, finally, the beggar: "I project my hat, sit shame-faced, and beg." This total embrace by Whitman of all humanity, and his identification with it—especially the flotsam and jetsam, the riffraff and rabble, the victimized and the outlawed—has repelled a few readers, even those disposed otherwise to appreciate *Leaves*. See especially the essay on Whitman in D. H. Lawrence's *Studies in Classic American Literature* (1923). But Whitman's universal embrace appears to be a genuine expression of his profound human—and democratic—sympathies, an empathetic realization in effect of the classic statement by the Latin dramatist Terence (ca. 190–159 B.C.): "I am a man: nothing human is alien to me."

It has been little noticed that Whitman's sexual sympathies flow out of his political themes. There are a number of passages in "Song of Myself" in which the poet presses his sexual embrace as energetically and indiscriminately as he presses his political. He says in the opening of Section 21:

I am the poet of the Body and I am the poet of the Soul,
The pleasures of heaven are with me and the pains of hell are with me,
The first I graft and increase upon myself, the latter I translate into a
    new tongue.

Later, in Section 24, he attempts the translation promised here:

I speak the pass-word primeval, I give the sign of democracy,
By God! I will accept nothing which all cannot have their counterpart
    of on the same terms.

Through me many long dumb voices,
Voices of the interminable generations of prisoners and slaves,
Voices of the diseas'd and despairing and of thieves and dwarfs,

Voices of cycles of preparation and accretion,
And of the threads that connect the stars, and of wombs and of the
    father-stuff,
And of the rights of them the others are down upon,
Of the deform'd, trivial, flat, foolish, despised,
Fog in the air, beetles rolling balls of dung.

Through me forbidden voices,
Voices of sexes and lusts, voices veil'd and I remove the veil,
Voices indecent by me clarified and transfigur'd.

I do not press my fingers across my mouth,
I keep as delicate around the bowels as around the head and heart,
Copulation is no more rank to me than death is.

I believe in the flesh and the appetites,
Seeing, hearing, feeling, are miracles, and each part and tag of me is
    a miracle.

Divine am I inside and out, and I make holy whatever I touch or am
    touch'd from,
The scent of these arm-pits aroma finer than prayer,
This head more than churches, bibles, and all the creeds.

This remarkable passage celebrating both sex and lust—clearly
linked to "the pass-word primeval" glossed as "the sign of democracy"—leads into an even more remarkable celebratory passage that
offers a mélange of sexual mixed with nature images suggesting a great
diversity of diffuse sexual feeling. The lines, exalting and magnifying
such feeling, might be read as the clarification and transfiguration of
those "voices indecent" promised by the poet. It is, as the first line
states, a proclamation of "worship" of the "spread" of the poet's
"own body, or any part of it." We might imagine the poet out in
nature alone suddenly and almost ecstatically beset by a sudden intense
awareness of his own sexuality, an awareness induced in part by
everything in the fecund natural setting that intermingles inextricably
with the overwhelming sense of sexual identity. The "firm masculine

colter" (an iron blade attached to a plowshare) is clearly the erect phallus, ready for the plowing and sowing in the act of tilling ("tilth"). The image of "milky stream pale strippings" of the poet's "life" is clearly suggestive of semen. Metaphors multiply thick and fast in the catalog of items the poet worships, each line ending with the emphatic "it shall be you!":

Root of wash'd sweet-flag! timorous pond-snipe! nest of guarded duplicate eggs! it shall be you!
Mix'd tussled hay of head, beard, brawn, it shall be you!
Trickling sap of maple, fibre of manly wheat, it shall be you!
Sun so generous it shall be you!
Vapors lighting and shading my face it shall be you!
You sweaty brooks and dews it shall be you!
Winds whose soft-tickling genitals rub against me it shall be you!
Broad muscular fields, branches of live oak, loving lounger in my winding paths, it shall be you!
Hands I have taken, face I have kiss'd, mortal I have ever touch'd, it shall be you.

What is dramatically presented in these lines is certainly not a sexual experience in the conventional sense, although fragments of previous experiences seem to surge up from the past. It is an imaginative state of sustained ecstasy equalling in intensity an orgasm—a transfiguring realization of one's sexual identity, and an intermingling of that identity with the outside world of nature. The sense of the sexual leads to, becomes inexplicably part of, the sense of the miraculous:

I dote on myself, there is that lot of me and all so luscious,
Each moment and whatever happens thrills me with joy,
I cannot tell how my ankles bend, nor whence the cause of my faintest wish,
Nor the cause of the friendship I emit, nor the cause of the friendship I take again.

That I walk up my stoop, I pause to consider if it really be,
A morning-glory at my window satisfies me more than the metaphysics of books.

"Song of Myself": Tapping Primal Energies

The poet unconsciously links his generalized and unfocused sexual feeling with feelings of the joy of being, the baffling mysteries of existence, and the obscure "cause" of friendship (the latter linkage an anticipation of Freudian theory discussed in chapter 6). In two climactic lines near the end of Section 24, the poet infuses the entire universe with overwhelming and sexual significance in a kind of transcendent cosmic copulation, dynamically orgasmic: "Something I cannot see puts upward libidinous prongs, / Seas of bright juice suffuse heaven."

Thus the sense of sexuality connects with the sense of awe, mystery, the miraculous, and the mystical, and with the pervasive theme of spirituality, which in a fundamental way provides for "Song of Myself" its loose structure. As we have seen, in some ways the structure of the poem can be considered cyclical, with themes introduced, dropped, reintroduced, and advanced—as in the movements of a symphony. But there is also a linear structure, with the poet embarked on a symbolic journey and arriving finally at a destination; the journey may be considered spiritual, and the destination the achievement of that mystical knowledge the journey itself has bestowed.

What is perhaps most extraordinary in this extraordinary poem is the union—at the beginning of the journey, especially as in Section 5, and again at the end of the journey in Section 50—of the sexual and spiritual imagery and themes that figure prominently throughout the poem. In Section 5, the poet's body seems to be embraced by his soul, both sexually and mystically:

I believe in you my soul, the other I am must not abase itself to you,
And you must not be abased to the other.

Loafe with me on the grass, loose the stop from your throat,
Not words, not music or rhyme I want, not custom or lecture, not
   even the best,
Only the lull I like, the hum of your valvèd voice.

I mind how once we lay such a transparent summer morning,
How you settled your head athwart my hips and gently turn'd over
   upon me,

And parted the shirt from my bosom-bone, and plunged your
    tongue to my bare-stript heart,
And reach'd till you felt my beard, and reach'd till you held my feet.

Swiftly arose and spread around me the peace and knowledge that
    pass all the argument of the earth,
And I know that the hand of God is the promise of my own,
And I know that the spirit of God is the brother of my own,
And that all the men ever born are also my brothers, and the
    women my sisters and lovers,
And that a kelson of the creation is love,
And limitless are leaves stiff or drooping in the fields,
And brown ants in the little wells beneath them,
And mossy scabs of the worm fence, heap'd stones, elder, mullein
    and poke-weed.

This is the moment of greatest concentration and tension in the
first part of "Song of Myself." Before this we have seen the poet,
with whom we have been asked to identify, abandoning his civilized
encumbrances and retreating to the woods to become "undisguised
and naked," and there to invite the experience that will bring comprehension of the mysteries that swarm through the poet's consciousness
(and unconscious), including the role of sex in the evolutionary unfolding of history:

Urge and urge and urge,
Always the procreant urge of the world.

Out of the dimness opposite equals advance, always substance and increase,
    always sex,
Always a knit of identity, always distinction, always a breed of life.

The experience comes in the form of a direct symbolic sexual union
of body and soul, a union that informs without the intervention of the
intellect of the "talkers," "trippers," and "askers" of the "creeds and
schools" or "houses and rooms" abandoned and held in abeyance for
a time. The soul, seizing the poet by his beard and feet and holding
him in a kind of entranced grip, opens his shirt to the "bosom-bone"

and penetrates with the tongue to the "bare-stript heart." In a kind of spiritual fellatio, the soul plunges tongue to heart, communing directly and ecstatically with it, where meanings are deeply *felt*, short-circuiting the intellect, where meanings are screened and obscured, befogged by the inadequacies of language.

Immediately the electrifying "peace and knowledge" that lie beyond intellect and argument flow from the soul through the body of the poet. What follows is the poet's groping about with inadequate language, tarnished by the "trippers and askers," to capture the elusive meaning of his ecstatic vision. It is a knowledge that somehow comprehends God, the brotherhood of men, the sisterhood of women, the humanhood of all, and the key itself: "a kelson of the creation is love." But the words fail to match the wonder of intuitive "truth," and the poet trails off in the end, launching a seemingly meaningless and incoherent catalog of the minutiae surrounding him in his natural setting—the "limitless" leaves "stiff or drooping in the fields," the "brown ants in the little wells," the "mossy scabs of the worm fence, heap'd stones, elder, mullein, and poke-weed." It is as though the poet, overwhelmed by such profound knowledge through his soul-searing experience, must cling to the immediate reality of a visible, touchable world to hold on to sanity.

As the voice of a child enters the poem at the beginning of Section 6, posing a question about the grass, and the poet begins a series of "guesses" as to what the grass means in an attempt to answer, he seems back on an even keel, ready to resume the journey, somehow spiritually invigorated and renewed after his transfiguring experience with his soul. At the beginning of Section 33, in its length, position, and substance a key transitional section of "Song of Myself," the poet exclaims:

Space and Time! now I see it is true, what I guess'd at,
What I guess'd when I loaf'd on the grass,
What I guess'd while I lay alone in my bed,
And again as I walk'd the beach under the paling stars of the morning.

My ties and ballasts leave me, my elbows rest in sea-gaps,
I skirt sierras, my palms cover continents,
I am afoot with my vision.

The poet's journey is a journey into knowing, and here we find him realizing that he has reached an important stage in that journey: the truth glimpsed beyond guessing. The reference in the second line seems to be a clear reference to his rendezvous with his soul in Section 5. Lines three and four suggest that there were other such experiences in a variety of environments, all of which left him in some sense earthbound. But now, after a multiplicity of insights poured forth in the Sections from 6 through 32, and particularly such experiences as that begun in Section 28 ("Is this then a touch? quivering me to a new identity?") and continued through Section 32, the poet is freed from his restraints, enlarged in imaginative grasp, and "afoot with [his] vision."

As Section 5 launched the poet's journey into knowing, and Section 33 defined one advanced stage in that journey, so Section 50 dramatizes the poet "coming out" of his ecstatic trance and concluding his journey:

> There is that in me—I do not know what it is—but I know it is in me.
>
> Wrench'd and sweaty—calm and cool then my body becomes,
> I sleep—I sleep long.
>
> I do not know it—it is without name—it is a word unsaid,
> It is not in any dictionary, utterance, symbol.
>
> Something it swings on more than the earth I swing on,
> To it the creation is the friend whose embracing awakes me.
>
> Perhaps I might tell more. Outlines! I plead for my brothers and
> sisters.
>
> Do you see O my brothers and sisters?
> It is not chaos or death—it is form, union, plan—it is eternal life—it
> is Happiness.

The "brothers and sisters" of these lines were introduced first in Section 5, as the poet searched for the language to embody his newly acquired knowledge. Thus it seems reasonable to see him, here, "coming out" of the state into which he was propelled by his body's encounter with his soul in that section.

The details of the lines in Section 50 suggest the emergence of the poet from the visionary state of a mystical trance (comparable to a transporting sexual experience): He is "wrench'd and sweaty," and then becomes "calm and cool," and enters a deep sleep, only to emerge with an excited sense of knowing. The experience has bestowed certitude of knowledge ("There is that in me—I do not know what it is—but I know it is in me"), but it has also bestowed frustration in that the knowledge eludes embodiment in words ("It is not in any dictionary, utterance, symbol"). Nevertheless, the poet—like many of the most dedicated mystics of the past—attempts to suggest the nature of the knowledge by trying out one tarnished word after another: "It is not chaos or death—it is form, union, plan—it is eternal life—it is Happiness."

What has led up to Section 50 that enables the poet to bring closure to his long poem-journey? The tone of oracular certainty that dominates the immediately preceding sections (48 and 49) begins in Section 38, one of the moments of clearest reversal in all of "Song of Myself":

Enough! enough! enough!
Somehow I have been stunn'd. Stand back!
Give me a little time beyond my cuff'd head, slumbers, dreams, gaping,
I discover myself on the verge of a usual mistake.

To encounter the ego dramatized in "Song of Myself" as being on the verge of a "usual mistake" should draw any reader up short. In the preceding sections, from about the middle of Section 33 through Section 37, the poet has been increasingly identifying with the degraded, downtrodden, and anguished to the point of becoming a beggar sitting shamefaced and extending his hat for alms. It is this and similar roles he has successively filled that he suddenly finds stifling and peremptorily casts off. Amidst a number of images related to crucifixion ("That

I could look with a separate look on my own crucifixion and bloody crowning"), the poet proclaims his resumption of the "overstaid fraction": "Corpses rise, gashes heal, fastenings roll from me." Remembering the renewal of resurrection to which the crucifixion led, the poet feels an infusion of spiritual energy enabling him to bring aid and comfort to those whose misfortunes and identities he had previously claimed as his own: "I troop forth replenish'd with supreme power, one of an average unending procession." In Section 40, the poet insists aggressively on sharing his newfound energy with all the world's "impotent"—or spirtually wounded and beaten:

> You there, impotent, loose in the knees,
> Open your scarf'd chops till I blow grit within you,
> Spread your palms and lift the flaps of your pockets,
> I am not to be denied, I compel, I have stores plenty and to spare,
> And any thing I have I bestow.

At the opening of Section 41, the poet subtly extends his mission to those who seemingly are self-sufficient: "I am he bringing help for the sick as they pant on their backs, / And for strong upright men I bring yet more needed help."

The nature of the poet's "supreme power," which he possesses in such abundance that he feels compelled to share it with others, is in his knowing, or in his way of self-confidently confronting the unknown. Throughout Sections 39–49, he shares that mystic power with the reader. In Section 44: "What is known I strip away, / I launch all men and women forward with me into the Unknown." In Section 45: "Every condition promulges not only itself, it promulges what grows after and out of itself, / And the dark hush promulges as much as any." In Section 46: "I know I have the best of time and space, and was never measured and never will be measured." In Section 47: "If you would understand me go to the heights or water-shore, / The nearest gnat is an explanation, and a drop or motion of waves a key." In Section 48: "I have said that the soul is not more than the body, / And I have said that the body is not more than the soul, / And nothing, not

God, is greater to one than one's self is." In Section 49: "And as to you Death, and you bitter hug of mortality, it is idle to try to alarm me." Throughout these and other lines of this closing phase of his journey, the poet exudes certitude and assurance in plenty on many of the matters that have puzzled and teased him in the earlier sections of "Song of Myself." They relate to universal and eternal questions of self and identity, love and friendship, life and death, God and eternity. And much of the poet's knowledge is in awareness of what he cannot know but must mystically intuit or divine.

In the closing two sections of "Song of Myself," 51 and 52, the poet turns from his groping attempt in Section 50 to find the word to summarize his knowledge and begins his farewell to the reader. In the process, in a number of vivid lines he obliquely characterizes the nature of what he has learned on his journey into knowing, alerting the reader to inconsistency: "Do I contradict myself? / Very well then I contradict myself, / (I am large, I contain multitudes.)" The knowledge is somehow primal, shared by the poet with the "spotted hawk": "I too am not a bit tamed, I too am untranslatable, / I sound my barbaric yawp over the roofs of the world." And the knowledge will continue to be elusive, though attainable indirectly, after the departure of the poet:

> I bequeath myself to the dirt to grow from the grass I love,
> If you want me again look for me under your boot-soles.

> You will hardly know who I am or what I mean,
> But I shall be good health to you nevertheless,
> And filter and fibre your blood.

In short, just as the readers must travel their own road, so they must by themselves discover the knowledge the journey brings. It must be earned; it cannot be given.

But after all, the poet's departure is by no means permanent. He says consolingly to the reader at the end: "Failing to fetch me at first keep encouraged, / Missing me one place search another, / I stop somewhere waiting for you." The poet *is* waiting for the reader, of course, in the sense that he is symbolically resurrected in the grass under the reader's boot soles, and is even—through his identity incarnate in the absorbed words of his book—inside the reader's skin, coursing through the reader's blood. But he is also waiting for the reader on the very next page, in an astonishing cluster of poems of procreation, "Children of Adam," which picks up a major theme of "Song of Myself" and carries it forward for the reader to explore more deeply.

6

The Omnisexual Vision of *Leaves*

Sexuality appeared as a theme in *Leaves of Grass* from the beginning, and in spite of the pressures Whitman felt periodically—from Ralph Waldo Emerson in 1860, from the Secretary of the Interior who fired Whitman from his job in 1865, and from the Society for the Suppression of Vice in 1881—he refused to remove the passages that some readers found offensive. And in his final assessment of his work in "A Backward Glance O'er Travel'd Roads," Whitman energetically defended the sexual themes as central to his purpose:

> *Leaves of Grass* is avowedly the song of Sex and Amativeness, and even Animality—though meanings that do not usually go along with those words are behind all, and will duly emerge; and all are sought to be lifted into a different light and atmosphere. Of this feature, intentionally palpable in a few lines, I shall only say the espousing principle of those lines so gives breath of life to my whole scheme that the bulk of those pieces might as well have been left unwritten were those lines omitted. Difficult as it will be, it has become, in my opinion, imperative to achieve a shifted attitude from superior men and women towards the thought and fact of sexuality, as an element in character, personality, the emotions, and a theme

in literature. I am not going to argue the question by itself; it does not stand by itself. The vitality of it is altogether in its relations, bearings, significance—like the clef of a symphony. At last analogy the lines I allude to, and the spirit in which they are spoken, permeate all *Leaves of Grass*, and the work must stand or fall with them, as the human body and soul must remain as an entirety. (452)

We have already seen how vital the sexual theme is in the scheme of "Song of Myself." It is dominant in the two clusters of poems that follow "Song of Myself": "Children of Adam" and "Calamus." These poems in sequence project the comprehensive nature of Whitman's omnisexual vision, and establish the case for its permeation of the whole of *Leaves of Grass*.

Whitman claimed that he made sexuality central to his book because in fact it was a vital element in "character, personality, the emotions," a claim that might be usefully examined in the light of similar claims by Sigmund Freud as he set them forth in *Civilization and its Discontents* (1930). Freud's conception of the interelationship of the individual and society is primarily sexual:

> Eros and Ananke [Love and Necessity] have become the parents of human civilization. . . . Man's discovery that sexual (genital) love afforded him the strongest experiences of satisfaction, and in fact provided him with the prototype of all happiness, must have suggested to him that he should continue to seek the satisfaction of happiness in his life along the path of sexual relations and that he should make genital erotism the central point of his life. . . . The love which founded the family continues to operate in civilization both in its original form, in which it does not renounce direct sexual satisfaction, and in its modified form as aim-inhibited affection. In each, it continues to carry on its function of binding together considerable numbers of people, and it does so in a more intensive fashion than can be effected through the interest of work in common.

Freud turned to the "careless way in which language uses the word 'love' " for demonstration of his point: "People give the name 'love' to the relation between a man and a woman whose genital needs have led them to found a family; but they also give the name 'love' to the positive feelings between parents and children, and between the brothers and sisters of a family, although *we* are obliged to describe this as 'aim-inhibited love' or 'affection.' "

Such "aim-inhibited love," Freud believed, was originally "fully sensual love, and it is so still in man's unconscious. Both—fully sensual love and aim-inhibited love—extend outside the family and create new bonds with people who before were strangers. Genital love leads to the formation of new families, and aim-inhibited love to 'friendships' which become valuable from a cultural standpoint because they escape some of the limitations of genital love, as, for instance, its exclusiveness."[1] There are many passages from *Leaves of Grass* called to mind by Freud's remarks here, but perhaps the most interesting are the concluding lines of a "Calamus" poem entitled "The Base of All Metaphysics":

> Having studied the new and antique, the Greek and Germanic systems,
> Kant having studied and stated, Fichte and Schelling and Hegel,
> Stated the lore of Plato, and Socrates greater than Plato,
> And greater than Socrates sought and stated, Christ divine having
>   studied long,
> I see reminiscent to-day those Greek and Germanic systems,
> See the philosophies all, Christian churches and tenets see,
> Yet underneath Socrates clearly see, and underneath Christ the divine I
>   see,
> The dear love of man for his comrade, the attraction of friend to friend,
> Of the well-married husband and wife, of children and parents,
> Of city for city and land for land.

What Whitman finds the base of all metaphysics Freud asserts as the base for all civilization. Both writers see society as founded on complex webs of love and friendship which in turn both see rooted in sexuality. The point to be made here is not that Whitman and Freud exhibit identical conceptions of the origin and nature of social bonds (they don't), but rather that both see significant connections between the psychosexuality of individuals and the society made up by bonds among those individuals.

Whatever Whitman's own personal sexual makeup and experience (and I suspect it is more complex than has yet been guessed), his imagination and vision were omnisexual. A believer in the "psychology" of his day, phrenology, Whitman was so proud of his phrenological reading—his "chart of bumps" (measuring the contours of the skull)—that he included it in one of those anonymous reviews he published of his first edition of *Leaves*. The chart demonstrated that two of his dominant traits were Amativeness and Adhesiveness, the first indicating the capacity for amorous relationships (procreational), the second for intimate friendships (comradeship).[2] Whitman often used these phrenological terms as code words in his prose and poetry when sketching his sexual themes.

He had the artist's capacity to imagine and recreate many sexual roles, and he showed an understanding of them and sympathy for them, and flung out his lines in celebration of them all—of sexuality in all its multiple forms as it bestowed being and identity on individuals and helped to form, mold, and shape relationships, societies, and nations. The sexual imagery of *Leaves of Grass* does not, to the dismay of its psychoanalytic readers, fall neatly into any single category. It is autoerotic, heteroerotic, homoerotic. Even more, it is projected beyond the human to the natural scene, and beyond nature to the cosmos, becoming cosmo-erotic. It permeates, as Whitman said, the whole book—the whole world that is created in *Leaves of Grass*.

In the opening poems of *Leaves of Grass*—"Song of Myself," "Children of Adam," and "Calamus"—the sexual imagery dominates by its sheer vitality and power. The autoerotic imagery comes to the fore in "Song of Myself," heterosexual imagery in "Children of Adam," and homosexual imagery in "Calamus." But in no case does one kind of imagery appear exclusively. There is much mingling and merging, and much sexual imagery that cannot be assigned to any one of these categories. Moreover, to identify the predominant imagery is not to locate the major significance—it is only the beginning. It is important at this point to recall Whitman's remark from "A Backward

Glance" that sexuality does not "stand by itself" but finds its vitality "altogether in its relations, bearings, significance—like the clef of a symphony." To call "Song of Myself," because of its abundant auto-erotic imagery, a poem about self-arousal and onanism would be a kind of madness. But to see the relationship between our sense of sexual identity and our conviction of selfhood, to see the part our primal energies play in shaping our being and becoming—that is to see the connections Whitman wanted to convey. To see "Children of Adam" as made up of heterosexual imagery and therefore devoted to male-female intercourse would be reductive in the extreme. The heterosexual imagery functions to suggest and imply something about the nature of human relationships, about the mystery of love, and about the miracle of procreation and the continuation in time beyond self of a part of self. To see "Calamus" as presenting homosexual imagery to describe male-male sexual relationships would be to read it with large blinders. To comprehend the homosexual imagery in its significance for genuine comradeship, for transexual human relationships, for brotherhood, for concepts of the democratic ideal is to comprehend it in the significance that Whitman clearly intended.

Identity, love, friendship—is there any other basis for conceiving a beginning for human society? These great themes are not, of course, original with Whitman, but his insistence on dramatizing their physical and sexual roots makes the themes peculiarly his in *Leaves of Grass*. His primary purpose was not to make personal revelations, but to proclaim to the world some truths about it and the beings who inhabit it that would not be explored in any depth by philosophers and scientists until the development of the "new psychology" by Freud and others at the end of the nineteenth century and the beginning of the twentieth. What the new psychologists were to "discover"—that sexuality permeated every aspect of human behavior and entered every phase of human relationships, male and female, in all their permutations—was something that Whitman had already proclaimed to the world in *Leaves of Grass*. But of course he had proclaimed much more in seeing the vitality of the all-pervasive sexuality in all its "relations, bearings, significance." If the opening of *Leaves of Grass* made manifest the sexuality that beat at the heart of being and becoming, of relating and connecting, the large remainder of *Leaves* assumed sexuality as the "clef" of the symphony, as the sounded key to which all life, the world, and the universe were attuned and to which they resonated.

When Whitman said, in "A Backward Glance," that the sexuality must remain in *Leaves of Grass* just as "the human body and soul must remain as an entirety," he was not exaggerating his case. The "enclosing" theme of *Leaves*, as Whitman variously and repeatedly described it, was its spiritual, or religious, theme. Over and over again in "Song of Myself," he insisted that the soul or spirit gained its identity only through the body (Section 3: "lacks one lacks both"). A similar relationship exists between the sexuality of *Leaves of Grass* and its spirituality. To remove the one would be to kill the book. And indeed, the soul takes its sustenance from that very sexuality that permeates every leaf.

Whitman stamps his major thematic premise in large letters all over *Leaves of Grass*. Here is an example, chosen at random, from "Starting from Paumanok" (Section 6):

> I will make the poems of materials, for I think they are to be the most
> spiritual poems,
> And I will make the poems of my body and of mortality,
> For I think I shall then supply myself with the poems of my soul and
> of immortality.

It cannot be stressed too much that such statements are not empty rhetoric or bravado boasting. They are a precise statement of plan and program, and they in effect describe what happens in the body (and soul) of *Leaves of Grass*.

We have observed that the dominant sexual imagery in "Song of Myself" is autoerotic, dramatizing the poet luxuriating in and celebrating his male sexual identity. An example, one of the most beautiful passages in the poem, appears in Sections 21–22:

> Press close bare-bosomed night—press close magnetic nourishing night!
> Night of south winds—night of the large few stars!
> Still nodding night—mad naked summer night.

The Omnisexual Vision of Leaves

Smile O voluptuous cool-breath'd earth!
Earth of the slumbering and liquid trees!
Earth of departed sunset—earth of the mountains misty-topt!
Earth of the vitreous pour of the full moon just tinged with blue!
Earth of shine and dark mottling the tide of the river!
Earth of the limpid gray of clouds brighter and clearer for my sake!
Far-swooping elbow'd earth—rich apple-blossom'd earth!
Smile, for your lover comes.

After imaginatively embracing both the night and the earth, the poet
seeks fulfillment in the sea:

You sea! I resign myself to you also—I guess what you mean,
I behold from the beach your crooked inviting fingers,
I believe you refuse to go back without feeling of me,
We must have a turn together, I undress, hurry me out of sight of the land,
Cushion me soft, rock me in billowy drowse,
Dash me with amorous wet, I can repay you.

This passage seems to be a literal fulfillment of Whitman's definition
of the poet's relationship to the world or cosmos: "The known universe
has one complete lover and that is the greatest poet" (1855 Preface,
416).

No doubt the most vivid images of autoerotic sexual arousal in
"Song of Myself" appear in Sections 28–29: "Is this then a touch?
quivering me to a new identity?" The imagery dramatizes sexual ecstasy moving to actual climax and release without introducing anyone
other than the poet present, but at the same time evokes a scene in
which the poet appears passive and pursued. The secret is Whitman's
dramatization of the senses in Section 28, all bribed to "swap off
with touch and go and graze at the edges" of the poet. These senses
("sentries") might have forestalled the encounter with "touch," but
they become traitors and let "touch" through to the "red marauder"
(the phallus erect):

The sentries desert every other part of me,
They have left me helpless to a red marauder,
They all come to the headland to witness and assist against me.

I am given up by traitors,
I talk wildly, I have lost my wits, I and nobody else am the greatest traitor,
I went myself first to the headland, my own hands carried me there.

You villain touch! what are you doing? my breath is tight in its throat,
Unclench your floodgates, you are too much for me.

Section 29 portrays the poet relaxed in the aftermath of orgasmic
release from his frenzied sexual intensities: "Blind loving wrestling
touch, sheath'd hooded sharp-tooth's touch! / Did it make you ache
so, leaving me?" Fragmentary, almost disembodied images appear
to float through the poet's mind, oblique embodiments or symbolic
projections of the ecstasies experienced:

> Parting track'd by arriving, perpetual payment of perpetual loan,
> Rich showering rain, and recompense richer afterward.
>
> Sprouts take and accumulate, stand by the curb prolific and vital,
> Landscapes projected masculine, full-sized and golden.

"Children of Adam," immediately following "Song of Myself" in
the *Leaves*, shifts the focus from the autoerotic to the heteroerotic,
just as "Calamus," following "Children of Adam," turns to the homoerotic. From the evidence of the manuscript, it is clear that Whitman
wrote the "Calamus" poems before writing those in "Children of
Adam." A manuscript note gives some sense of his motivation in
placing the two clusters of poems together in his masterwork:

> Theory of a Cluster of Poems the same *to the passion of Woman-
> Love* as the *Calamus-Leaves* are to adhesiveness, manly love.
>   Full of animal-fire, tender, burning,—the tremulous ache, deli-
> cious, yet such a torment.
>   The swelling elate and vehement, that will not be denied.
>   Adam, as a central figure and type.[3]

The "Children of Adam" cluster begins and ends with dramatic mono-
logues, in which Adam addresses Eve, the two accepting their sexual

natures and identity with joyous affirmation. It is this sexual ideal—
the relationship of Adam and Eve before the Fall—that is to be re-
claimed and celebrated in the poem-cluster.

The second poem of the cluster, "From Pent-up Aching Rivers,"
is a programmatic poem serving as a kind of table of contents for the
main images of the cluster. The poet announces that he will be "singing
the phallus, / Singing the song of procreation." And he will be explicit
in his celebration of male-female love:

> The female form approaching, I pensive, love-flesh tremulous aching,
> The divine list for myself or you or for anyone making,
> The face, the limbs, the index from head to foot, and what it
>   arouses,
> The mystic deliria, the madness amorous, the utter abandonment.

Probably the most impressive passage of heterosexual imagery in
all of "Children of Adam" appears in "I Sing the Body Electric," in
the middle of the poet's "divine list" or catalog of the female body:

> Mad filaments, ungovernable shoots play out of it [the female form],
>   the response likewise ungovernable,
> Hair, bosom, hips, bend of legs, negligent falling hands all diffused,
>   mine too diffused,
> Ebb stung by the flow and flow stung by the ebb, love-flesh swelling
>   and deliciously aching,
> Limitless limpid jets of love hot and enormous, quivering jelly of love,
>   white-blow and delirious juice,
> Bridegroom night of love working surely and softly into the prostrate
>   dawn,
> Undulating into the willing and yielding day,
> Lost in the cleave of the clasping and sweet-flesh'd day.

The poet's celebration of the human body, both male and female, and
his celebration of heterosexuality and procreation are accompanied by
an insistence on a dimension beyond the physical: "O I say these are
not the parts and poems of the body only, but of the soul, / O I say now
these are the soul!" Throughout "Children of Adam," a revitalized

and robust heterosexuality is envisioned as providing the means for renewal and for return to the natural relationship of the sexes that existed between Adam and Eve before the Fall: "The garden the world anew ascending."

In "Calamus" Whitman announced in his very title the image that dominates the cluster—the phallus as it is suggested by the phallic-shaped calamus or sweet flag, either in its spears or its roots. It is perhaps useful to recall that Whitman has already, in "Song of My-self," given the image sexual connotations (in Section 24, in the middle of a catalog of nature-sex images): "Root of wash'd sweet-flag! timo-rous pond-snipe! nest of guarded duplicate eggs!" It is impossible to read the "Calamus" poems under the domination of that phallic image without associating the emotions expressed with homosexual feelings and longings—and it is equally impossible not to believe that Whitman intended this association. In "These I Singing in Spring," the poet explicitly identifies the calamus root with the love of comrades:

And here what I now draw from the water, wading in the pond-side,
(O here I last saw him that tenderly loves me, and returns again never to
separate from me,
And this, O this shall henceforth be the token of comrades, this
calamus-root shall,
Interchange it youths with each other! let none render it back!)

If the phallic-like calamus root image permeates the entire cluster of poems, as I suggest it does, then such a poem as "When I Heard at the Close of the Day" becomes clearly a poem of homosexual love consummated. It is a poem describing separation and then reunion, and the reunion brings fulfillment:

And that night while all was still I heard the waters roll slowly continually
up the shores,
I heard the hissing rustle of the liquid and sands as directed to me
whispering to congratulate me,
For the one I love most lay sleeping by me under the same cover in the
cool night,

In the stillness in the autumn moonbeams his face was inclined toward
  me,
And his arm lay lightly around my breast—and that night I was happy.

This narrative of love fulfilled is not typical of "Calamus." As fre-
quently as not, the poet's passion is secret and silent and unreturned.
Typical of this kind of poem is "O You Whom I Often and Silently
Come":

O you whom I often and silently come where you are that I may be
  with you,
As I walk by your side or sit near, or remain in the same room with
  you,
Little you know the subtle electric fire that for your sake is playing
  within me.

That the "Calamus" emotion is one with which the poet struggled
is made quite explicit in "Earth, My Likeness":

Earth, my likeness,
Though you look so impassive, ample and spheric there,
I now suspect that is not all;
I now suspect there is something fierce in you eligible to burst forth,
For an athlete is enamour'd of me, and I of him,
But toward him there is something fierce and terrible in me eligible to
  burst forth,
I dare not tell it in words, not even in these songs.

It would seem obtuse, in view of the omnipresent calamus-phallic
image, not to recognize the nature of the male-male attraction in this
poem. But this danger of total physical commitment, which might be
seen as lurking in all sexuality, whatever its manifestation, is balanced
by the potentiality expressed again and again throughout "Calamus"
of transfiguring the calamus emotion into a social sentiment that cre-
ates and binds a society—as in the lines quoted earlier from "The Base
of All Metaphysics." In brief, just as autoeroticism and heterosexuality
can be reduced to mere carnality and lust, so can homosexuality. But

as autoeroticism can be seen as a basis for identity and definition of being, and heterosexuality as the basis for a vital and renewed relationship between the sexes (genuine love), so homosexuality can be transfigured into the social ideal of the love between comrades and of democratic brotherhood.

Most people, we now know, are compounded emotionally of all three sexualities, some having more of one component, others more of another. Whitman was one of the first to recognize and explore in depth the complexities and possibilities of sexual feeling with the comprehensiveness of an omnisexual vision. A writer of the twentieth century, also endowed with similar vision—D. H. Lawrence— summed Whitman up in this way:

> What a great poet Whitman is: great like a great Greek. For him the last enclosures have fallen, he finds himself on the shore of the last sea. The extreme of life: so near to death. It is a hushed, deep responsibility. And what is the responsibility? It is for the new great era of mankind. And upon what is this new era established? On the perfect circuits of vital flow between human beings. First, the great sexless normal relations between individuals, simple sexless friendships, unison of family, and clan, and nation, and group. Next, the powerful sex relation between man and woman, culminating in the eternal orbit of marriage. And, finally, the sheer friendship, the love between comrades, the manly love which alone can create a new era of life.[4]

Did Whitman speak more for men than for women; was he a prisoner of his maleness? The answer might come from a variety of sources. There is, for example, the sensitive feminine nineteenth-century response to Whitman recorded in Ann Gilchrist's "An Englishwoman's Estimate of Walt Whitman" (1870), in which she bestowed lavish praise on "Song of Myself," "Children of Adam," and "Calamus."[5] And there is the later appreciation by Kate Chopin, shown by her use of Whitman's sexual imagery in her fiction, as, for example, her use of a Whitman quotation at a thematically critical moment in "A Respectable Woman"—the line leading into one of the poet's most sensuous passages in Section 21 of "Song of Myself": "Night of South Winds—night of the large few stars! / Still nodding night—"[6] And there are innumerable passages in *Leaves of Grass* that deserve closer scrutiny as they relate to feminine identity, for example, the account of the 28-year-old woman imaginatively bathing with the 28 nude young men in Section 11 of "Song of Myself," or the story of the poet's mother and her "Calamus"-like attachment to a red squaw described in "The Sleepers." These and other passages must be examined to determine whether Whitman fulfilled his proclamation in Section 21 of "Song of Myself": "I am the poet of the woman the same as the man, / And I say it is as great to be a woman as to be a man."

7

Wandering the Open Road

Having achieved physical/sexual/mystical birth in "Song of Myself" and plumbed to the base of "all metaphysics" (that is, the hidden sexual roots) of love, friendship, community, and civilization in "Children of Adam" and "Calamus," Whitman next wanders out on the open road to greet the world: "Salut au Monde!" and "Song of the Open Road" lead off the "song section" of *Leaves of Grass*, a collection of 11 medium-length poems on various subjects and themes. They are often referred to as the "song section" because of the recurring appearance of the word *song* in their titles. Following this section, and allied thematically to it, are the cluster "Birds of Passage," the topical poem "A Broadway Pageant," and two additional clusters, "Sea-Drift" and "By the Roadside." These poems and clusters bring us up to the major shift in focus in the heart and center of *Leaves of Grass*, "Drum-Taps," inspired by that key transfiguring event in America's nineteenth century, the Civil War.

It is useful to begin this part of Whitman's book by glancing at the words and images introduced in the titles of the 11 poems of the song section: "Salut au Monde!," "Song of the Open Road," "Crossing Brooklyn Ferry," "Song of the Answerer," "Our Old Feuillage," "A Song of Joys," "Song of the Broad-Axe," "Song of the Exposition,"

"Song of the Redwood-Tree," "A Song for Occupations," and "A Song of the Rolling Earth." The repeated use of the word *song* in the titles suggests the celebratory nature of these poems, and the image of the world in the first and last suggests something of their reach: The poet begins by saluting the world, and ends with hailing its continuation on *its* journey through the universe. In the opening poems, travel images dominate, but the emphasis shifts in the later poems to the specific occasions or subjects inspiring the songs—joys, the broad-axe, an exposition, the redwood-tree, occupations, the "rolling earth."

Although a number of these poems stand out as among Whitman's most interesting experiments—"Song of the Open Road," "Song of the Broad-Axe," "Song of the Redwood-Tree," for instance—there can be no doubt that his greatest success, and a poem that must be counted among a handful of Whitman's masterpieces, is "Crossing Brooklyn Ferry." Here as elsewhere in *Leaves of Grass*, Whitman has astutely sorted and arranged his poems so that they have some resemblance to a mountain range, with one or two peaks rising higher than the others and dominating the surrounding landscape so as to command attention and offer challenge. "Crossing Brooklyn Ferry" is just such a poem and richly repays exploration in depth. It gathers to itself with great thematic force the pattern developed throughout the songs, dramatizing the experience of the poet in dynamic and probing encounters with the world—and especially America—in its varied symbolic settings and scenes. The poem begins with the mundane experience of taking a ride on a ferryboat to get from one side of a river to another, but soon opens out to consideration of the most baffling mysteries of being, living, communing, and sharing.

"Crossing Brooklyn Ferry" was called "Sun-Down Poem" when it first appeared in the 1856 edition of *Leaves of Grass*. It is revealing to consider why Whitman might have changed the title. Although the poem opens at sundown, it is by no means about a time of day. By beginning his title with a nonfinite form of the verb, "crossing," he immediately establishes the ambiguity of the time of the action the verb describes, embracing as it does past, present, and future. By naming a specific boat, Brooklyn Ferry—carrying commuters over the East River between Brooklyn and Manhattan—Whitman immediately evokes not only the flowing water of the river but also crowd and city scenes, all of which connect significantly with his thematic purposes. (The ferry was replaced later in the nineteenth century by Brooklyn Bridge, which inspired Hart Crane's *The Bridge*, 1930, in which Whitman figures as a kind of American muse.)

"Crossing Brooklyn Ferry" introduces two major characters, the speaker and You, the reader. The poem is ingeniously structured so as to bring the speaker closer and closer to the reader, reaching ultimately a moment of most intimate sharing. You the reader are introduced in the last line of Section 1: "And you that shall cross from shore to shore years hence are more to me, and more in my meditations, than you might suppose." Then, You the reader emerge as a central figure in the opening seven lines of Section 3, reincarnating the feelings and repeating the actions of the poet who crossed before You in a series of lines beginning "Just as you": "Just as you stand and lean on the rail, yet hurry with the swift current, I stood yet was hurried." In Section 4, You appear in the opening line, and You seem to be the one meant for assignation in the ambiguous and parenthetical last line (the parentheses establish the tone of an intimate aside to You): "(The time will come, though I stop here to-day and to-night.)"

In the opening two lines of Section 5, the "I" and the "You" in the poem merge for the first time into "us": "What is it then between us? / What is the count of the scores or hundreds of years between us?" You remain an important presence throughout Section 6, and You suddenly find yourself sensing the intrusion into your private space of the constantly moving and shifting poet: "Closer yet I approach you, / . . . Who knows, for all the distance, but I am as good as looking at you now, for all you cannot see me?" The climax of this "plot" of "Crossing Brooklyn Ferry" comes in lines 5–6 of the penultimate Section 8: "What is more subtle than this which ties me to the woman or man that looks in my face? / Which fuses me into you now, and pours my meaning into you?" Section 8 then ends with the teasing lines:

We understand then do we not?
What I promis'd without mentioning it, have you not accepted?

What the study could not teach—what the preaching could not
accomplish is accomplish'd, is it not?

What is it that "we" now understand? What was promised, but not
mentioned? What is it that has been taught and accomplished that
neither teaching nor preaching could teach or accomplish? These questions go to the heart of the poem's elusive meaning, and the answers
may refuse to settle into the worn, tarnished words of the language at
our command.

But before considering these questions, there is the prior question
as to how the poet achieved his fusion with the reader in the poem. In
Section 1, the poet is verbally in his own present ("I see . . .") and You
are in the future tense ("And you that shall cross . . ."). In Section 2,
the first group of lines is actually a catalog of substantives, without
finite verbs establishing a time; the second group of lines all refer to
the future ("Others will enter. . . . / Others will watch . . . / Others will
see . . ."). The poet makes a gigantic leap with his verbs in Section 3,
moving to the present with You the reader ("I am with you, you men
and women of a generation, or ever so many generations hence"), and
seems to enter the reader's present tense, fathoming his or her feelings
and thoughts and looking back on his life enclosed in the past ("Just
as you feel when you look on the river and sky, so I felt"). In Sections
4, 5, and 6, the poet remains in the reader's present tense, the two of
them looking back in time to the poet's life in the past. In Sections 7
and 8, the poet begins an intimate sharing with the reader, climaxed
in lines 5–6 of Section 8: "What is more subtle than this which ties
me to the woman or man that looks in my face? / Which fuses me into
you now, and pours my meaning into you?" The intimate tone is
unmistakable, and the metaphoric sexual suggestiveness ("fuses me
into you," "pours my meaning into you") inescapable. The intimate
rendezvous promised to the reader in the aside of Section 4 ("The time
will come, though I stop here to-day and to-night") has indeed been
fulfilled.

Something of a beginning of an answer as to what the poet assumes (in Section 8) the reader to have understood from this experience
might be found in Section 9, the closing section of the poem. The verb

form that dominates is the imperative, with the poet directly addressing each item in a long catalog recapitulating all the images of the poem that have heretofore figured in the poet's and reader's shared experience of crossing on the ferry: "Flow on, river! flow with the flood-tide, and ebb with the ebb-tide! / Frolic on, crested and scallop'd-edg'd waves!" Among the objects addressed are a number that seem especially suggestive of transcendent meaning: "Throb, baffled and curious brain! throw out questions and answers!"; "Suspend here and everywhere, eternal float of solution!"; "Receive the summer sky, you water, and faithfully hold it till all downcast eyes have time to take it from you!"; "Diverge, fine spokes of light, from the shape of my head, or anyone's head, in the sunlit water!" The long catalog constituting the first group of lines of Section 9 concludes:

> You necessary film, continue to envelop the soul,
> About my body for me, and your body for you, be hung our divinest
>   aromas,
> Thrive, cities—bring your freight, bring your shows, ample and
>   sufficient rivers,
> Expand, being than which none else is perhaps more spiritual,
> Keep your places, objects than which none else is more lasting.

     Section 5 contains some important lines that relate to a number of the lines just quoted:

> I too had been struck from the float forever held in solution,
> I too had receiv'd identity by my body,
> That I was I knew was of my body, and what I should be I knew I
>   should be of my body.

When "solution" is reintroduced in the catalog of Section 9, it is given an expanded context: "Suspend here and everywhere, eternal float of solution!" What does it mean to be "struck from the float forever held in solution"? The "solution" appears to be a chemical metaphor for the transcendent liquid in which the divine source-stuff of matter is held diffused and suspended—until the objects and beings of the world are precipitated from it, achieving physical form. Thus the origins of the poet and of the poet's companion "You," as well as of all the items in the catalog, may be traced back to this sacred source. All have achieved identity by their physical being, and thus their physical identity provides the basis for their spiritual identity—those "divine aromas"—as well. Whitman had written in Section 3 of "Song of Myself": "Clear and sweet is my soul, and clear and sweet is all that is not my soul. / Lack one lacks both. . . ."

In the closing lines of Section 9 the poet addresses the objects listed in the preceding catalog as "dumb, beautiful ministers":

We use you, and do not cast you aside—we plant you permanently
  within us,
We fathom you not—we love you—there is perfection in you also,
You furnish your parts toward eternity,
Great or small, you furnish your parts toward the soul.

By absorbing the images of the world—planting them "permanently" within—the poet and reader have intuited the unity they share which their separate identities superficially deny. All have been struck from the solution; all will return to the solution. "Crossing Brooklyn Ferry" may be seen, then, as a counterbalance to "Song of Myself," focusing not on the separateness of the self but rather on the identity and unity of the En-Masse.

It is this sense of unity underlying all the world's diversity that appealed to Henry David Thoreau and inspired him to ask Whitman, when he visited the poet in 1856, whether he had read the sacred Oriental texts. Whitman's reply, "No. Tell me about them," should not be taken at face value.[1] He would have known about such texts, if in no other way, through reading Emerson. Emerson's most famous image, which relates closely to—but differs significantly from—the theme of "Crossing Brooklyn Ferry," appears in his first book, *Nature* (1836):

In the woods, we return to reason and faith. There I feel that nothing can befall me in life,—no disgrace, no calamity (leaving me my

71

eyes), which nature cannot repair. Standing on the bare ground,—
my head bathed by the blithe air, and uplifted into infinite space,—
all mean egotism vanishes. I become a transparent eyeball; I am
nothing; I see all; the currents of the Universal Being circulate
through me; I am part or parcel of God. The name of the nearest
friend sounds then foreign and accidental: to be brothers, to be
acquaintances, master or servant, is then a trifle and a disturbance.
I am the lover of uncontained and immortal beauty. In the wilder-
ness, I find something more dear and connate than in streets or
villages. In the tranquil landscape, and especially in the distant line
of the horizon, man beholds somewhat as beautiful as his own
nature.[2]

Emerson's "currents of the Universal Being" and Whitman's "eternal
float of solution" have remarkably similar metaphorical thrusts. That
Emerson needed the solitude of undisturbed nature to sense the unity
underlying all diversity, and that Whitman could experience that unity
in the midst of crowds gathered together on a ferryboat or tramping
the streets of the city, indicates the distance separating the poetic
materials to which they gravitated. But there seems little distance separating the transcendent truths they both believed they intuited.

• • •

In contrast with the song section's focus on encounter with the world,
"Birds of Passage," "A Broadway Pageant," "Sea-Drift," and "By the
Roadside" appear to focus in one way or another on time, particularly
as it is introduced in the first poem of "Birds of Passage," "Song of
the Universal":

> In spiral routes by long detours,
> (As a much-tacking ship upon the sea,)
> For it [the soul] the partial to the permanent flowing,
> For it the real to the ideal tends.
>
> For it the mystic evolution,
> Not the right only justified, what we call evil also justified.

"A Broadway Pageant" portrays the visit of two Japanese envoys to Manhattan in June 1860 as symbolic of the end of the westward movement of humankind from its place of origin in the Orient:

Were the children straying westward so long? so wide the tramping?
Were the precedent dim ages debouching westward from Paradise so long?
Were the centuries steadily footing it that way, all the while, unknown, for
you, for reasons?

Whitman considers the otherwise unremarkable event as completing another cycle in "mystic evolution," fulfilling some obscure but vital purpose embracing him, America, and You the reader.

In "Sea-Drift," the poems become filled with more personal reference, and the lead poem, "Out of the Cradle Endlessly Rocking," is a kind of memory poem, a recollection of the key experience in the poet's boyhood that determined him to become a poet. In "By the Roadside," the poet seems to have become something of a passive observer, and miscellaneous poems abound—brief and simple "Thoughts" side by side with "A Farm Picture" and "A Child's Amaze"; the cluster concludes with "To the States [To Identify the 16th, 17th, or 18th Presidentiad]," a vituperative picture of the three vacillating presidencies leading up to 1860 and the Civil War. It is noteworthy that the titles "Birds of Passage," "A Broadway Pageant," "Sea-Drift," and "By the Roadside" evoke images of air, city, sea, and land (or countryside) and that they move in the main from larger to lesser cycles or units of time, until, in "By the Roadside," the poet seems drawing to an end and full stop before the abrupt shift and new departure in the Civil War cluster that follows.

The one undeniable masterpiece in this part of the *Leaves* is "Out of the Cradle Endlessly Rocking," reflecting the theme of time in its very title, whether we consider the metaphor of the rocking cradle (the endless renewal of the cycle-bound human race) or the image for which the rocking cradle is metaphor—the waves of the sea—which dates back to the dim beginnings of creation itself. In portraying a key event of his distant past—his boyhood—the poet thus dramatizes how the past endures in the present and shapes the future.

Because "Out of the Cradle" tends by its dramatic tensions and emotional intensity to hold the interest of the reader, it may usefully serve for exploration of some of the vital elements of Whitman's poetic technique. It is generally acknowledged that Whitman's richly inventive ways of using free verse constituted one of his most radical and innovative contributions to poetry. One of the finest examples of his ingenuity in its use is in the opening 31 lines of "Out of the Cradle Endlessly Rocking." These lines are perhaps the best realization in all *Leaves of Grass* of Whitman's ideal of organic form, the natural fusion of form and substance, the one supporting and giving emphasis to the other at every turn.

The first 22 lines form the opening single sentence of the poem. To be experienced to the fullest this passage must be read aloud, with attention to its subtle cadences. For it is a mistake to think of verse that is "free" as lacking rhythm or rhyme: When written by a master like Whitman, free verse is incredibly rich in both. It does not adopt a fixed metrical system, rhyme scheme, or stanzaic pattern. But it is certainly free to use a variety of meters, diverse rhyming or "sound echoing" techniques, and varied groupings of lines that reflect natural units of thought or feeling expressed by the poem. Even the flowing lines themselves, as they lengthen or shorten, may form rhythmic shapes on the page.

Before reading the lines aloud, it is useful to recreate—imaginatively—the dramatic situation we find at the opening of "Out of the Cradle Endlessly Rocking." A lone man sits by himself, perhaps in a twilight room full of shadows, sinking into a revery of times past; fragments of a crucial boyhood experience begin to float through his mind, hovering around him, swarming over him, flooding through him so as finally to carry him out of himself and back in time to relive that moment of his boyhood that defined his inspiration and enduring identity as a poet. As you read the lines aloud, listen to their subtle cadences as they convey meaning and emotion simultaneously:

Out of the cradle endlessly rocking,
Out of the mocking-bird's throat, the musical shuttle,

Out of the Ninth-month midnight,
Over the sterile sands and the fields beyond, where the child leaving his bed
    wander'd alone, bareheaded, barefoot,
Down from the shower'd halo,
Up from the mystic play of shadows twining and twisting as if they were
    alive,
Out from the patches of briers and blackberries,
From the memories of the bird that chanted to me,
From your memories sad brother, from the fitful risings and fallings I
    heard,
From under that yellow half-moon late-risen and swollen as if with tears,
From those beginning notes of yearning and love there in the mist,
From the thousand responses of my heart never to cease,
From the myriad thence arous'd words,
From the word stronger and more delicious than any,
From such as now they start the scene revisiting,
As a flock, twittering, rising, or overhead passing,
Borne hither, ere all eludes me, hurriedly,
A man, yet by these tears a little boy again,
Throwing myself on the sand, confronting the waves,
I, chanter of pains and joys, uniter of here and hereafter,
Taking all hints to use them, but swiftly leaping beyond them,
A reminiscence sing.

This astonishing passage accomplishes so much in so little space that it is literally breathtaking. There is only one sentence, but what a sentence! It is, technically, a "periodic" sentence, suspending completion of meaning throughout until the very end. The subject of the sentence appears at the beginning of the antepenultimate line, the verb as the last word of the last line, and the objective complement the next-to-last word of the last line: "I sing a reminiscence." All the remaining lines of the passage may be connected as modifiers to this short sentence.

Where does the music of the passage come from? We cannot count all of the ways, but we may discover some. Take, for example, the first line and rewrite it: "Out of the rocked cradle." Does this revision jar the ear? Whitman originally wrote the line thus, and then revised it to its present form: "Out of the Cradle Endlessly Rocking," which may

be scanned: "Oút ŏf thĕ Crádlĕ // Éndlĕsslў Róckĭng." We might observe that the metrical feet employed are a dactyl followed by a trochee
in each of the two halves of the line. By his revision, Whitman also
slowed the line a bit by introducing a pause in the middle (a caesura),
and he changed the action from the past-tense "rocked" to the adjecti-
val gerund "rocking," that is, from finished to ongoing. And he gave
emphasis to the on-going-ness by modifying it with the mellifluous
"endlessly" (note the hard "d" and the liquid sounds of the "l" echoing
the same sounds in "cradle"). So much for one line. But these observa-
tions do not carry us very far with the other lines: such is the nature
of free verse.

Instead of looking at the ends of lines for rhyme, we might glance
at the beginnings. The first 15 lines of the passage begin with preposi-
tional phrases: three lines beginning with "out of the," then one each
beginning "over the," "down from the," "up from the," "out from
the," and then eight lines beginning with "from," varied thus: "from
the," "from your," "from under," "from those," "from the," "from
the," "from the," "from such." The effect of the initial repetitions of
sounds and structures is complex: There are music and emphasis in the
exact rhymes, of course. As images from the past press in from every
direction (out, over, down, up, from), the poet seems unable to extri-
cate himself from the entangled and entangling swarm of fragmentary
memories and submits himself to them, relives the experience imaginatively, and embodies it as relived in the very poem we are reading:

> From the myriad thence-arous'd words,
> From the word stronger and more delicious than any,
> From such as now they start the scene revisiting,
> As a flock, twittering, rising, or overhead passing,
> Borne hither, ere all eludes me, hurriedly,
> A man, yet by these tears a little boy again,
> Throwing myself on the sand, confronting the waves. . . .

"Out of the Cradle Endlessly Rocking" was once entitled "A
Word Out of the Sea," suggesting that the experience was in some
sense linguistic, the discovery of a fate-determining word; we know
from reading the end of the poem that its riddle-solving and mystically

final word whispered by the sea is "death." The fragments of memory become for the poet the "myriad thence-arous'd words," which in turn become like a "flock" of "twittering" birds, flying back into the past to revisit the scene and carrying with them as one of their own the tearful poet's gravity-defying imagination that enables him to become "a little boy again" on the seashore, "confronting the waves" and the soul-transforming word those waves temporarily conceal but will shortly reveal in their hiss. The metaphor of the flock of birds is, of course, a foreshadowing of the tragic love-drama of the two mocking-birds.

The opening lines of "Out of the Cradle Endlessly Rocking" reveal that the reminiscer is not only a poet but also a poet who is a "chanter of pains and joys, uniter of here and hereafter," a poet who takes "all hints to use them, but swiftly [leaps] beyond them." As we relive with the poet his boyhood experience, listening first to the he-bird's celebratory song of joyous love, and then, after the mysterious disappearance of the she-bird at sea, to the he-bird's mournful carol of "lonesome love," we feel that we are on the verge of hearing some vital yet still secret revelation. After the last notes of the bird's song are "translated" by the poet, he pours out a summary descriptive passage that is both a virtuoso performance in the rich musical cadences of free verse and a deep-diving quest for meaning that will not yield to similar translation:

The aria sinking,
All else continuing, the stars shining,
The winds blowing, the notes of the bird continuous echoing,
With angry moans the fierce old mother incessantly moaning,
On the sands of Paumanok's shore gray and rustling,
The yellow half-moon enlarged, sagging down, drooping, the face of
    the sea almost touching,
The boy ecstatic, with his bare feet the waves, with his hair the
    atmosphere dallying,
The love in the heart long pent, now loose, now at last tumultuously
    bursting,
The aria's meaning, the ears, the soul, swiftly depositing,
The strange tears down the cheeks coursing,
The colloquy there, the trio, each uttering,

The undertone, the savage old mother incessantly crying,
To the boy's soul's questions sullenly timing, some drown'd secret
   hissing,
To the outsetting bard.

Present participles end each line except the last, and sometimes appear within the line, giving us the equivalent of a long sequence of end-rhymes. But the effect is more complex: The repeated "ing" words bestow an on-going-ness on the experience, eternalizing it in effect for the poet, rendering it unforgettable in the way we have just seen at the beginning of the poem, where we witnessed the poet overwhelmed by memory and carried back through time to relive the experience. Moreover, the lengthy repetition of the present participles, concentrating in themselves all the "action" of the passage, highlights their suggestive imagery: sinking, continuing, shining, blowing, echoing, moaning, rustling, sagging, drooping, touching, dallying, bursting, depositing, coursing, uttering, crying, timing, hissing. Read together, apart from their context, the words are highly charged sexually, some even vaguely orgasmic, perhaps obliquely conveying the nature of the "actual" experience for which the birds are used for symbolic distancing.

It is interesting in this regard to glance for a moment at another Whitman passage similar in many ways, found in Section 26 of "Song of Myself":

A tenor large and fresh as the creation fills me,
The orbic flex of his mouth is pouring and filling me full.

I hear the train'd soprano (what work with hers is this?)
The orchestra whirls me wider than Uranus flies,
It wrenches such ardors from me I did not know I possess'd them,
It sails me, I dab with bare feet, they are lick'd by the indolent waves,
I am cut by bitter and angry hail, I lose my breath,
Steep'd amid honey'd morphine, my windpipe throttled in fakes of death,
At length let up again to feel the puzzle of puzzles,
And that we call Being.

Wandering the Open Road

The poet hears the sounds of deeply moving music (the soprano is operatic, the bird's song an "aria"), responds ecstatically and physically, with many of the attributes of the response similar to sexual climax. There is also in both passages the imagery of the poet's feet caressed by the waves of the sea, as there is a strong sense of some supreme knowledge withheld ("puzzle of puzzles," "drown'd secret").

The boy in "Out of the Cradle Endlessly Rocking," however, has gained partial knowledge from the experience of listening to the he-bird's carol of "lonesome love," as indicated in the line: "The aria's meaning, the ears, the soul, swiftly depositing." The knowledge is not intellectual but spiritual, absorbed not by the mind but by the "soul" where it is "deposited swiftly," that is, directly. (Compare this to Section 5 of "Song of Myself," in which the soul's tongue plunges directly to the poet's heart.) The trio participating in the "colloquy" in this passage is made up of the he-bird with his song, the boy with his "soul's questions," and the sea ("the savage old mother") hissing her "drown'd secret." But the secret will out at the end of the poem. The boy pleads for the "clew" that has been withheld, appealing to the sea: "Are you whispering it, and have been all the time, you sea-waves? / Is that it from your liquid rims and wet sands?" The sea relents:

> Whereto answering, the sea,
> Delaying not, hurrying not,
> Whisper'd me through the night, and very plainly before daybreak,
> Lisp'd to me the low and delicious word death,
> And again death, death, death, death,
> Hissing melodious, neither like the bird nor like my arous'd child's heart,
> But edging near as privately for me rustling at my feet,
> Creeping thence steadily up to my ears and laving me softly all over,
> Death, death, death, death, death.

By the language of his body in response to the waves, the boy reveals that the knowledge of death is in some sense sexual knowledge. The waves approach "hissing," suggestive of the serpent, in turn suggestive of the phallus; but the "hissing" is not dissonant (or frightening), but "melodious." The sea approaches the boy like a lover and holds him in sexual embrace—not unlike the embrace of the body by the soul in Section 5 of "Song of Myself." In both instances the individual emerges from the experience *knowing*. Thus the "clew" stands revealed, but it is not in simply knowing the Word but in experiencing the Word as conveyed by the sea.

In the closing lines of the poem, as the poet traces his birth as a poet back to the experience narrated ("My own songs awaked from that hour"), he connects the sea metaphorically with his title, "Out of the Cradle Endlessly Rocking": ("Or like some old crone rocking the cradle, swathed in sweet garments, bending aside"). He has already referred to the sea as "the savage old mother incessantly crying." This image of a rocking cradle is of course the image of birth and life (appropriate for the sea, the source of life), and yet the same waves that are the rocking cradle become also the voice to utter or whisper the "delicious word death," conveyed simultaneously with an ecstatic, quasi-sexual embrace. By such juxtapositions, the poet subterraneously connects sex and birth with death. The one is in some obscure way the other, the two merged thus inseparably in the poet's songs. In the opening lines of "Out of the Cradle Endlessly Rocking," the mature poet described himself as "chanter of pains and joys, uniter of here and hereafter." He shows himself a master of these themes in the poem, first in translating the he-bird's song of joy, followed by his song of pain, and next by uniting the visual image of the rocking cradle with the sound image of the Word from the sea ("Death") in the sea-waves "endlessly" rocking and whispering. Birth and death are obscurely interlinked, the one inevitably and inextricably implicit in the other.

8

The Real Parturition Years of America

When Whitman first published *Drum-Taps* in 1865, he thought (as he revealed in a letter to W. D. O'Connor, 6 January 1865) that he had left *Leaves of Grass* behind as his first book, accomplishing his aim "to express by sharp-cut self assertion, *One's Self* & also, or may be still more, to map out, to throw together for American use, a gigantic embryo or skeleton of Personality,—fit for the West, for native models." And he believed that he was then embarked on a different if complementary book: "I am perhaps mainly satisfied with *Drum-Taps* because it delivers my ambition of the task that has haunted me, namely, to express in a poem (& in the way I like, which is not at all by directly stating it) the pending action of this *Time & Land we swim in*, with all their large conflicting fluctuations of despair & hope, the shiftings, masses, & the whirl & deafening din, (yet over all, as by invisible hand, a definite purport & idea)—with the unprecedented anguish of wounded & suffering, the beautiful young men, in wholesale death & agony, everything sometimes as if in blood color, & dripping blood" (*Corres.* 1:246–47).

When Whitman wrote these words, the Civil War was not yet ended and Abraham Lincoln had not been assassinated. But he seems to have seen that America, through the purging of the war, had now the possibility of fulfilling the promise of its beginning, the promise of the Declaration of Independence whose ringing sentences on freedom ("all men are created equal") had rung hollow in the face of the preservation of slavery. He would later (in "A Backward Glance") see the Civil War years as the real "parturition," or birth, years of the country, providing him firsthand with the epic materials he had longed for when he had started out many years before to be the poet of America and democracy.

As expressed in the same January 1865 letter to W. D. O'Connor, Whitman felt that his *Drum-Taps* poems were an advance in his art both in form and substance. He wrote of the new work: "It is in my opinion superior to *Leaves of Grass*—certainly more perfect as a work of art, being adjusted in all its proportions, & its passion having the indispensable merit that though to the ordinary reader let loose with wildest abandon, the true artist can see it is yet under control." As to the substance and effect of *Drum-Taps*, Whitman wrote: "The book is . . . unprecedently [*sic*] sad, (as these days are, are they not?)—but it also has the blast of the trumpet, & the drum pounds & whirrs in it, & then an undertone of sweetest comradeship & human love, threading its steady thread inside the chaos, & heard at every lull & interstice thereof—truly also it has clear notes of faith & triumph" (*Corres.* 1:246–47).

Not many critics would agree with Whitman that in *Drum-Taps* he had exceeded the art of *Leaves of Grass* as it stood in the 1860 edition. But there is general critical consensus that Whitman's Civil War poems, especially after the inclusion of "When Lilacs Last in the Dooryard Bloom'd" in subsequent issues of *Drum-Taps*, constitute the greatest body of poetry inspired by that tragic but nationally transforming struggle. The only other poetry that merits comparison with it is Herman Melville's *Battle-Pieces and Aspects of the War,* published in 1866. Melville's use of traditional metrical and stanzaic patterns gives his poetry a constrained appearance when compared with the passionate free-verse poems of Whitman, but American literature is enriched by both bodies of poetry written by two of the country's greatest nineteenth-century writers.

The Real Parturition Years of America

By the time Whitman observed in "A Backward Glance" that it was only from "the strong flare and provocation" of the Civil War's "sights and scenes" that he had discovered the "final reasons-for-being of an autochthonic and passionate song," he had already integrated the Civil War poems into his masterwork, *Leaves of Grass*, where they occupied the great heart and center. When he also observed that without "those three or four years and the experiences [of the war] they gave, *Leaves of Grass* would not now be existing," he surely had reference to the book as the American epic it had become by the time of its final shaping in 1881. Deep down Whitman felt that his work up to the Civil War had drawn largely on his own intuitive self as a democratic individual and on the abstract and intangible theory of America and its democracy. Somehow the terrible struggle of the Civil War made concrete and tangible the country and its ideals, and reinvigorated and authenticated his role as its epic poet. He was, in short, witness to, and played his part in, America's *real* birth.

The events of the Civil War are the central points of reference in "Drum-Taps" and "Memories of President Lincoln," of course, but its shadow (the war's aftermath) is cast far beyond these clusters in the book, extending through "By Blue Ontario's Shore" and "Autumn Rivulets." The impact of the war on Whitman may be gauged by his feeling the necessity after the war of revising "By Blue Ontario's Shore," the poem he had shaped in 1856 from his 1855 prose preface. The preface had implicitly set forth his ambitious poetic plans through enumerating the attributes of the ideal American poet, or "poet of the kosmos." The early versions of "By Blue Ontario's Shore" incorporated many phrases and sentences verbatim from the preface, and reflected its optimistic tone. The tone of the post-war version was less confident but filled with a deeper sense of urgency, portraying the muse as a "Phantom gigantic superb, with stern visage" demanding a "song of the throes of Democracy."

The dominant poem in "Autumn Rivulets" is "The Return of the Heroes," which is about the soldiers (those who survived) going home from the battlefields and settling into their civilian roles and routines. It sets the direction for the other miscellaneous poems in the cluster, culled from many different editions of *Leaves of Grass*, which Whitman seemed to believe captured the temper, moods, and activities of the country after the war (even though a number of them had been written before it).

The first thing to observe about "Drum-Taps" is that the poems are not written out of one fixed emotional reaction to the war but out of the entire spectrum of feelings and attitudes that the poet felt during the four-year course of the struggle. There is, in the opening poems, an excited welcoming of the war, almost a celebration of it as the nation rushes into battle. "First O Songs for a Prelude," with its celebratory tone, is clearly written by one who does not know war at first hand:

War! an arm'd race is advancing! the welcome for battle, no turning away;
War! be it weeks, months, or years, an arm'd race is advancing to
    welcome it.

Mannahatta a-march—and it's O to sing it well!
It's O for a manly life in the camp.

Whitman might have dropped these lines as being out of harmony with the poems he wrote after seeing the battlefields. But he wanted to be faithful to emotions as they were actually experienced, not as they might be revised by hindsight. He might have said of his method in "Drum-Taps" what he had said about his earlier work in that 1865 letter to O'Connor: "I see now, [there are] some things in it I should not put in if I were to write now, but yet I shall certainly let them stand, even if but for proofs of phases passed away—" (*Corres.* 1: 247).

The celebratory tone of "Drum-Taps" gradually fades away as the poet draws closer to the war, particularly in those "snapshots" or vignettes of actual war scenes: "Cavalry Crossing a Ford," "Bivouac on a Mountain Side," "An Army Corps on the March," and "By the Bivouac's Fitful Flame." It is interesting to note that the varied scenes do not include scenes of actual battle or its aftermath. But immediately after these four short descriptive poems, "Come Up from the Fields

Father" appears, depicting a scene on the domestic front in which an Ohio farm family receives the news by letter that their soldier-son has been wounded; the poet, revealing that the son is actually dead, portrays the bewilderment and sorrow the family experiences in the loss of an only son. From this point on, the dominant tone of "Drum-Taps" turns somber, melancholy, and at times mournful, as though the meaning of war has finally come home to the poet.

Following "Come Up from the Fields Father," the poet shifts his focus from the farm fields to the battlefields with "Vigil Strange I Kept on the Field One Night." The narrative, the first set on the battlefield with a participant-narrator, is given in that "undertone of sweetest comradeship & human love" Whitman mentioned in his letter to O'Connor. It is perhaps the most moving poem in all of "Drum-Taps." The soldier-speaker returns to his fallen comrade, finds him dead, and spends the night there on the battlefield with him: "Vigil of silence, love and death, vigil for you my son and my soldier, / As onward silently stars aloft, eastward new ones upward stole." Then, as morning comes, the speaker ritualistically buries his comrade:

Till at latest lingering of the night, indeed just as the dawn appear'd,
My comrade I wrapt in his blanket, envelop'd well his form,
Folded the blanket well, tucking it carefully over head and carefully
    under feet,
And there and then and bathed by the rising sun, my son in his
    grave, in his rude-dug grave I deposited,
Ending my vigil strange with that, vigil of night and battle-field dim,
Vigil for boy of responding kisses, (never again on earth
    responding,)
Vigil for comrade swiftly slain, vigil I never forget, how as day
    brighten'd,
I rose from the chill ground and folded my soldier well in his
    blanket,
And buried him where he fell.

Note that the narrative in effect concludes with the fourth line of this passage, describing the burial of the dead comrade; but the poem goes on for five more lines, telling us what we already know, even repeating phrases that we have heard before. But these last lines are perhaps the poem's most effective in their requiem-like cadences, in the slowed drumbeat of the fragmentary meters, in the echoing repetitions of words and phrases. By intoning them slowly and soberly as accompaniment to the ritual of burial, the soldier seems readier to come to terms with his deep grief.

After the companion poems "Come Up from the Fields Father" and "Vigil Strange I Kept on the Field One Night," the suffering and agony of the wounded and dying—and the shock of the living—dominate the poetry, as is seen in such effective poems as "A March in the Ranks Hard-Prest, and the Road Unknown," "A Sight in Camp in the Daybreak Gray and Dim," "As Toilsome I Wander'd Virginia's Woods," "The Wound-Dresser," "Dirge for Two Veterans," "Over the Carnage Rose Prophetic a Voice," and "The Artilleryman's Vision" (a remarkable dramatization of a soldier reliving in his dreams the chaos and confusion of his battlefield experience).

As we near the end of "Drum-Taps," with the war now over, all of the exultation at the start of the war heard in the beginning poems of the cluster has disappeared. Instead the poet's thoughts turn repeatedly to death, and his sympathies are extended even to the enemy, as in the remarkably effective poem "Reconciliation":

Word over all, beautiful as the sky,
Beautiful that war and all its deeds of carnage must in time be utterly lost,
That the hands of the sisters Death and Night incessantly softly wash
    again, and ever again, this soil'd world;
For my enemy is dead, a man divine as myself is dead,
I look where he lies white-faced and still in the coffin—I draw near,
Bend down and touch lightly with my lips the white face in the coffin.

This note of reconciliation is sounded repeatedly in the closing poems. And in a poem entitled "Lo, Victress on the Peaks," clearly written in celebration of victory (the triumph of "Libertad," another name for "Victress"), the poet characterizes his war poems thus: "No poem proud, I chanting bring to thee, nor mastery's rapturous verse, / But a cluster containing night's darkness and blood-dripping wounds, / And psalms of the dead."

One of these dead is, of course, Abraham Lincoln, and his death is the subject of the cluster following "Drum-Taps," "Memories of President Lincoln." The section contains only four poems, but two of these are among the most famous Whitman ever wrote. Both are elegies for Lincoln. "When Lilacs Last in the Dooryard Bloom'd" was written in Whitman's characteristic free-verse style; "O Captain! My Captain!" was written in a highly uncharacteristic fixed stanzaic pattern with a set rhyme scheme and metrical pattern. It is ironic that for a long time "O Captain! My Captain!" was far more popular than any other poem by Whitman, including his other elegy on Lincoln, which by general critical consent is among his greatest works, and certainly the best to come out of the Civil War years.

"When Lilacs Last in the Dooryard Bloom'd" does not mention Lincoln by name, but associates him with the western star, as it associates the grief of the poet with the lilacs, and the source of spiritual awareness with the hermit thrush. In weaving these three extraordinary symbols through the poem in a kind of cyclic movement, Whitman achieves effects peculiarly his. But with all its innovation in style and form, "When Lilacs Last in the Dooryard Bloom'd" is a traditional elegy in its structure. It begins, in Section 2, by expressing an almost inconsolable grief for the dead president:

> O powerful western fallen star!
> O shades of night—O moody, tearful night!
> O great star disappear'd—O the black murk that hides the star!
> O cruel hands that hold me powerless—O helpless soul of me!
> O harsh surrounding cloud that will not free my soul.

Note that many of the short, exclamatory constructions are incomplete, and that all of the lines and some of the half-lines begin with "O" (like the form of the lips in grief). The tone is that of a semidisciplined lament about to break into an uncontrollable wail.

By the end of the poem (as in the traditional elegy), the poet has become reconciled to the death that at the beginning had caused such grief. Section 16 of "When Lilacs Last in the Dooryard Bloom'd" can only be called a virtuoso performance in free verse, with lines casting a powerful, hypnotic-like spell over the engaged reader; they are among the greatest Whitman ever wrote:

Passing the visions, passing the night,
Passing, unloosing the hold of my comrades' hands,
Passing the song of the hermit bird and the tallying song of my soul,
Victorious song, death's outlet song, yet varying ever-altering song,
As low and wailing, yet clear the notes, rising and falling, flooding the
    night,
Sadly sinking and fainting, as warning and warning, and yet again bursting
    with joy,
Covering the earth and filling the spread of the heaven,
As that powerful psalm in the night I heard from recesses,
Passing, I leave thee lilac with heart-shaped leaves,
I leave thee there in the door-yard, blooming, returning with spring.

I cease from my song for thee,
From my gaze on thee in the west, fronting the west, communing with thee,
O Comrade lustrous with silver face in the night.

Yet each to keep and all, retrievements out of the night,
The song, the wondrous chant of the gray-brown bird,
And the tallying chant, the echo arous'd in my soul,
With the lustrous and drooping star with the countenance full of woe,
With the holders holding my hand nearing the call of the bird,
Comrades mine and I in the midst, and their memory ever to keep, for the
    dead I loved so well,
For the sweetest, wisest soul of all my days and lands—and this for his
    dear sake,
Lilac and star and bird twined with the chant of my soul,
There in the fragrant pines and the cedars dusk and dim.

The tone is contemplative, wistfully accepting, imbued with a subdued joy tinged with melancholy. The ritualistic, incantatory repetitions of words and phrases have an effect similar to that produced by the latter part of "Vigil Strange I Kept on the Field One Night." The focus has shifted from the shock at the loss of Lincoln in the opening of the poem to the fond recollection of him and the memory of the experience with the hermit thrush, bringing reconciliation to death at the end.

According to these closing lines, the solitary poet was paradoxically accompanied by two comrades, one on either side and the three holding hands; they listened to the bird's "victorious song," "death's outlet song of life"; and the poet's soul echoed a "tallying chant"—in effect the elegy we are reading.

Tension in the poem is created by the poet's initial resistance to the call of the hermit thrush to come to the swamp cedars. He is held back by the "thought of him I love"—and the necessity he feels to express his love by bestowing the lilacs on his coffin. The bird calls to him in Section 4, again in Section 9, and still again in Section 13. At last, the ritual of his grief played out, in Section 14 the poet obeys the call:

Then with the knowledge of death as walking one side of me,
And the thought of death close-walking the other side of me,
And I in the middle as with companions, and as holding the hands of
    companions,
I fled forth to the hiding receiving night that talks not,
Down to the shores of the water, the path by the swamp in the dimness,
To the solemn shadowy cedars and ghostly pines so still.

The comrades, then, are metaphors, one for the "thought of death" (that love for the living Lincoln, and the loss felt on his death), the other for the "sacred knowledge of death" (comprehension of the deepest spiritual meaning of death, which the poet intuits and the hermit thrush articulates in his song). The image of the three comrades holding hands in effect is a symbolic representation of the reconciliation to the bitter loss—or thought—of death by the "sacred knowledge" of its release, its transfiguration into birth. The bird's song, as tallied by the poet, addresses death as "lovely and soothing," and calls death the "dark mother" and the "strong deliveress." Listening to the bird, the poet in Section 15 discovers within himself a kind of inner vision: "While my sight that was bound in my eyes unclosed, / As to long panoramas of visions." What he sees is that "the slain soldiers of the war" were "not as was thought," but "themselves were fully at rest" and "suffer'd not."

It says something about the durability of the appeal of Whitman's

Civil War poems that they were often quoted on radio (as read and recorded by the actor Ralph Bellamy) during World War II (1939–45), another war that witnessed the death of a president, Franklin D. Roosevelt, just as the war was approaching its end. And on the assassination of President John Kennedy in 1963, "When Lilacs Last in the Dooryard Bloom'd" was read on radio and television as an expression of the national grief widely and deeply felt. It is no small tribute to these poems that they could fill what was perceived as a public need some one hundred years after they were written. Whitman surely would have found the reading of his poems on such solemn public occasions to express the feelings of the people as a fulfillment of his poetic intention to become the poet of America and its democracy.

In the opening of "By Blue Ontario's Shore," the poet once again encounters the muse—as he did at the opening of *Leaves of Grass* in the second poem of "Inscriptions," "As I Ponder'd in Silence." In the earlier poem, the muse was an Old World muse, accusatory, demanding that the poet write of battles, wars, and heroic soldiers. The poet had to fall back on the claim that his subject was, metaphorically, what the muse demanded ("*I too haughty Shade also sing war, and a longer and greater one than any, / Waged in my book with varying fortune, with flight, advance and retreat, victory deferr'd and wavering*"). The muse of "By Blue Ontario's Shore," no longer the "genius of poets of old lands," is America's own muse, earned by the fighting of the Civil War. But this New World muse has more than the war in mind as the poet's subject:

By blue Ontario's shore,
As I mused of these warlike days and of peace return'd and the dead that
　　return no more,
A Phantom gigantic superb, with stern visage accosted me,
*Chant me the poem, it said, that comes from the soul of America, chant me
　　the carol of victory,*
And strike up the marches of Libertad, marches more powerful yet,
And sing me before you go the song of the throes of democracy.

(Democracy, the destin'd conqueror, yet treacherous lip-smiles everywhere,
And death and infidelity at every step.)

The Real Parturition Years of America

It is instructive to compare Whitman's 1855 Preface and "By Blue Ontario's Shore," noting the revisions and the shifts in emphasis he made in delineating the role and function of the American poet. In both works he insisted on the necessary relationship between the poet and his time. In the 1855 Preface he wrote: "The direct trial of him who would be the greatest poet is today. If he does not flood himself with the immediate age as with vast oceanic tides . . . and if he does not attract his own land body and soul to himself and hang on its neck with incomparable love and plunge his semitic muscle into its merits and demerits . . . and if he be not himself the age transfigured . . . and if to him is not opened the eternity which gives similitude to all periods and locations and processes and animate and inanimate forms, and which is the bond of time . . .—let him merge in the general run and wait his development" (424–25). This startling passage was included, with some changes, in Section 6 of "By Blue Ontario's Shore" in a description of the American bard—

> incarnating this land,
> Attracting it body and soul to himself, hanging on its neck with
>   incomparable love,
> Plunging his seminal muscle into its merits and demerits,
> Making its cities, beginnings, events, diversities, wars, vocal in him,
> Making its rivers, lakes, bays, embouchure in him. . . .

Whitman's image of the American bard embracing his country as lover and "plunging his seminal muscle into its merits and demerits" is astonishing, not to say shocking ("semitic" became "seminal" in the revision). The figure suggests Whitman's intuitive awareness of sexual energy as source not only for the poet's lyric creativity but also for his epic ambition or responsibility, inspiring his probing of the nation's virtues as well as its faults. Moreover, using such explicit sexual union with the whole country as a metaphor for the bardic function becomes highlighted in its poetic form.

The poet who has become the "age transfigured," who has come to incarnate "this land," can say with Whitman in Section 17 of "By Blue Ontario's Shore" (in lines that did not appear in the 1855 Preface):

O I see flashing that this America is only you and me,
Its power, weapons, testimony, are you and me,
Its crimes, lies, thefts, defections, are you and me,
Its Congress is you and me, the officers, capitols, armies, ships, are you
    and me,
Its endless gestations of new States are you and me,
The war, (that war so bloody and grim, the war I will henceforth
    forget), was you and me,
Natural and artificial are you and me,
Freedom, language, poems, employments, are you and me,
Past, present, future, are you and me.

Poets who believe themselves to have become America in this Whitmanian sense have their justification for writing their lyric-epics in which they set themselves forth as their own heroes: They are ready, as Ezra Pound said of Whitman, to go "bail for the nation." The poets who have come after Whitman and have devoted their energies and talents to the construction of their own lyric-epics, have not all appeared to "go bail for the nation," but they have appeared eager to plunge their "seminal muscles" into America's merits and demerits, sometimes as an act of love, sometimes in rapacious assault.

Anyone wishing to track closely Whitman's development as a poet will find rich materials in comparing the 1855 Preface and "By Blue Ontario's Shore," paying close attention to which lines were salvaged from the essay and the new contexts into which they were placed in the poem. "By Blue Ontario's Shore" also might bear comparison with "Starting from Paumanok," which serves for the first part of *Leaves of Grass* something of the same function that "By Blue Ontario's Shore" serves for this second or middle part. Both are in some sense mythic biographies, although the earlier poem is focused more on the self, the second on America. "Starting from Paumanok" appears to be a more unified and powerful poem, in part no doubt because of the prominent role given to You, the reader, as the poet's intimate camerado ready to accompany him on the journey he is beginning.

"Autumn Rivulets," the final cluster of the heart and center of

Leaves of Grass, suggests its nature in the opening lines of the opening poem, *"As Consequent, Etc."*:

> As consequent from store of summer rains,
> Or wayward rivulets in autumn flowing,
> Or many a herb-lined brook's reticulations,
> Or subterranean sea-rills making for the sea,
> Songs of continued years I sing.

The diversity of the poems gathered in this section is suggested by the variations Whitman devises for his water-metaphor: "autumn rivulets," "herb-lined" brooks, "subterranean sea-rills." What we might expect, then, is something less ambitious than major rivers or great lakes (we have just come from Ontario's shore). Nevertheless, a number of the short poems of the cluster are extraordinarily fine, including "There Was a Child Went Forth," "This Compost," "Sparkles from the Wheel," "Unfolded Out of the Folds," and "My Picture-Gallery."

The one long poem with significant connection to the Civil War, "The Return of the Heroes," the second poem in the cluster, was in an earlier appearance (*Two Rivulets*, 1876) preceded by a headnote: "In all History, antique or modern, the grandest achievement yet for political Humanity—grander even than the triumph of THIS UNION over Secession—was the return, disbanding, and peaceful disintegration from compact military organization, back into agricultural and civil employments, of the vast Armies, the two millions of embattled men of America—a problem reserved for Democracy, our day and land, to promptly solve."[1] The poem, first called "A Carol of Harvest for 1867," portrays the demobilized soldiers returning to their homes and helping in the autumn harvest. In Section 4 of the poem, the poet, seemingly almost against his will, lingers over images of the just-finished war:

When late I sang sad was my voice,
Sad were the shows around me with deafening noises of hatred and smoke
    of war;

In the midst of the conflict, the heroes, I stood,
Or pass'd with slow step through the wounded and dying.

But now I sing not war,
Nor the measur'd march of soldiers, nor the tents of camps,
Nor the regiments hastily coming up deploying in line of battle;
No more the sad, unnatural shows of war.

Some of the most powerful lines of the poem embody images of the suffering soldiers on the battlefield, but the poet admonishes himself to turn from the war scenes: "But on these days of brightness, / On the far-stretching beauteous landscape, the roads and lanes, the high-piled farm-wagons, and the fruits and barns, / Should the dead intrude?" It is worthy of note that in "The Return of the Heroes" Whitman once again introduces and elaborates the title image of his book (see especially Section 6 of "Song of Myself"), as in the closing of an idyllic rural description at the end of Section 7, where it is described lyrically as "the good green grass, that delicate miracle the ever-recurring grass."

9

Bridging the Way from Life to Death

After "Autumn Rivulets," we enter the third and final part of the main structure of *Leaves of Grass*, gathering together many of the poems (but others also) that Whitman once considered as destined for a separate volume entitled *Passage to India*. His ideas about such a volume were set forth in his Preface to *Two Rivulets* (1876), Volume II of the so-called Centennial Edition of *Leaves of Grass*: "It was originally my intention, after chanting in *Leaves of Grass* the songs of the Body and Existence, to then compose a further, equally needed Volume, based on those convictions of perpetuity. . . . I meant . . . to shift the slides, and exhibit the problem and paradox of the same ardent and fully appointed Personality entering the sphere of the re-sistless gravitation of Spiritual Law, and with cheerful face estimating Death, not at all as the cessation, but as somehow what I feel it must be, the entrance upon by far the greatest part of existence, and something that Life is at least as much for, as it is for itself." The poems to which he refers, he said, contain "thoughts, or radiations from thoughts, on Death, Immortality, and a free entrance into the Spiritual world" (434).

It is the function of "Proud Music of the Storm," which immedi-

95

ately follows "Autumn Rivulets," to announce these very themes. "Proud Music" is a dream poem in which the poet hears as in a vision the entire sweep of the world's music from the prehistory period to the present (including numerous operas). In the last section of the poem, the poet wakes and, full of an intuitive knowledge, addresses his soul:

> I said to my silent curious soul out of the bed of the slumber-chamber,
> Come, for I have found the clew I sought so long,
> Let us go forth refresh'd amid the day,
> Cheerfully tallying life, walking the world, the real,
> Nourish'd henceforth by our celestial dream.

The poet then informs his soul that the sounds heard during the dream were not what they appeared to be, "But to a new rhythmus fitted for thee, / Poems bridging the way from Life to Death, vaguely wafted in night air, uncaught, unwritten, / Which let us go forth in the bold day and write."

The third and final thematic grouping of poems and poem-clusters in *Leaves of Grass* includes: "Proud Music of the Storm," "Passage to India," "Prayer of Columbus," "The Sleepers," "To Think of Time," and "Whispers of Heavenly Death." The two major poems in this part of *Leaves* are "Passage to India" and "The Sleepers." The first of these was published in 1871, and marks the end chronologically of the somewhat long list of Whitman's poems that have by a number of critics been declared masterpieces. "The Sleepers" was, in its first version, published in the 1855 edition of *Leaves of Grass* and has gradually taken its place alongside "Song of Myself," "Crossing Brooklyn Ferry," "Out of the Cradle Endlessly Rocking," "When Lilacs Last in the Dooryard Bloom'd," and "Passage to India" as one of Whitman's major achievements.

"Passage to India" begins by celebrating the major engineering achievements of the mid-nineteenth century that have accomplished the circling of the globe: the Suez Canal (completed in 1869), the transatlantic cable (completed in 1866), and the transcontinental railroad (completed in 1869 with the joining of the Union Pacific and Central Pacific at Promontory Point, Utah). In Whitman's imagination, these achievements had brought humankind in its restless western movement from the place of its origin in the Orient around the earth to California's shores and the Pacific Ocean—which if traversed would bring the migration back to the point of its beginnings: "modern science" had made possible a return to the past and the realm of "deep diving bibles and legends." "Passage to India" calls for the imaginative leap by the soul to a symbolic India, with spiritual achievements to match those of a wondrous technology.

From the scenes of the present day's scientific achievements in Section 3, the poem begins in Section 4 a transcendent view of world history that has led to the moment the poet celebrates in the nineteenth century: "Along all history, down the slopes, / As a rivulet running, sinking now, and now again to the surface rising, / A ceaseless thought, a varied train—lo, soul, to thee, thy sight, they rise." Section 5 represents the mythic view of history, beginning with Adam and Eve and their "myriad progeny" from the "gardens of Asia descending radiating," "Wandering, yearning, curious, with restless explorations." The section concludes with a radical redefinition of the Christian Trinity: "Trinitas divine shall be gloriously accomplish'd and compacted by the true son of God, the poet, / . . . Nature and Man shall be disjoin'd and diffused no more, / The true son of God shall absolutely fuse them." In Section 6, traditional history of the history books is given its due, with an outpouring of the names of explorers and discoverers, but the leading role is given to Christopher Columbus:

> As the chief histrion,
> Down to the footlights walks in some great scena,
> Dominating the rest I see the Admiral himself,
> (History's type of courage, action, faith).

Beginning in Section 7, the poet turns from the historic explorers to a call for the soul's own voyage and "circumnavigation of the world," its return "to primal thought," to "realms of budding bibles," to "reason's early paradise," to "wisdom's birth, to innocent intu-itions, / Again with fair creation." All is preparation for the poet, in his soaring imagination, to set sail with his soul in Section 8, the poem's climactic representation of mystical union with God, who is addressed in ecstatically visionary terms:

> O Thou transcendent,
> Nameless, the fibre and the breath,
> Light of the light, shedding forth universes, thou centre of them,
> Thou mightier centre of the true, the good, the loving,
> Thou moral, spiritual fountain—affection's source—thou reservoir.

In this passage, the poet moves swiftly from one metaphor to another in the attempt to characterize the uncharacterizable, using much of the language of a long line of traditional mystics who have sought union with God: "the fibre," "the breath," the "mightier centre of the true, the good, the loving," a "spiritual fountain" and "reservoir." In prepa-ration for the imaginative union, the poet must call upon his soul, his "actual" self, to make expansive preparation for such an overwhelm-ing encounter:

> Swiftly I shrivel at the thought of God,
> At Nature and its wonders, Time and Space and
>   Death,
> But that I, turning, call to thee O soul, thou actual Me,
> And lo, thou gently masterest the orbs,
> Thou matest Time, smilest content at Death,
> And fillest, swellest full the vastnesses of Space.

With his soul magnified to mate "Time" and fill the "vastnesses of Space" (the traditional barriers all mystics must overcome in their yearning to merge with the Transcendent), the poet is ready for the union.

But the encounter with God, though dramatically represented, is projected into the future, to come after the poet's death:

Bridging the Way from Life to Death

> Reckoning ahead O soul, when thou, the time achiev'd,
> The seas all cross'd, weather'd the capes, the voyage done,
> Surrounded, copest, frontest God, yieldest, the aim attain'd,
> As fill'd with friendship, love complete, the Elder Brother found,
> The Younger melts in fondness in his arms.

Here the poet's imaginative conception of God ("Elder Brother") differs radically from those distancing metaphors he has previously used in direct address. Indeed, the metaphor for union with God is drawn from the central emotion portrayed in the poet's "Calamus" poems, here a kind of transcendent—and supremely fulfilled—adhesiveness. In this final merge, with the Younger Brother melting in the arms of the Elder Brother, there is the deep soul-sharing in masculine embrace for which the poet has yearned and which he has idealized throughout his life.

Section 9, the final section of "Passage to India," portrays the poet calling for his soul to set sail, impatient for the journey to experience the union he has anticipated in imagination:

> Sail forth—steer for the deep waters only,
> Reckless O soul, exploring, I with thee, and thou with me,
> For we are bound where mariner has not yet dared to go,
> And we will risk the ship, ourselves and all.

There is in this passage the urge not only to get on with the journey toward God but also to explore on that journey "the deep waters only"—where may be found clues for "bridging the way from Life to Death" for poems yet to be written. The British novelist E. M. Forster felt the power of Whitman's poem compelling enough to inspire him to adopt the title for his last and finest novel, *Passage to India* (1924), which embodied many of the themes of *Leaves of Grass* in its narrative set in modern India. This silent appropriation says much about the high valuation this leading British writer placed on the American poet.

"Prayer of Columbus," which follows "Passage to India," is most interesting for its portrayal, in the form of a dramatic monologue (or soliloquy), of that figure in American history who had repeatedly been projected by ambitious poets as a potential epic hero. Columbus, as we have seen, makes an appearance in "Passage to India," playing his role as the "chief histrion" in his discovery of the New World. In "Prayer of Columbus," we find him near the end of his life, a "batter'd, wreck'd old man," not unlike Whitman himself in 1874, when the poem was written. Readers have tended to identify Whitman with the speaker of the poem, and with good reason. Whitman himself once commented to a friend about the poem: "As I see it now I shouldn't wonder if I have unconsciously put a sort of autobiographical dash in it."[1] Columbus, addressing God about his life's work, seems to reinforce such an identification:

> All my emprises have been fill'd with Thee,
> My speculations, plans, begun and carried on in thoughts of
>   Thee,
> Sailing the deep or journeying the land for Thee;
> Intentions, purports, aspirations mine, leaving the results to Thee.

The poem, one of the finest short poems in *Leaves*, was first printed with a headnote when published in the 1876 volume, *Two Rivulets*. This headnote is useful in revealing Whitman's intention and in helping readers to comprehend the poem:

> It was near the close of his indomitable and pious life—on his last voyage when nearly 70 years of age—that Columbus, to save his two remaining ships from foundering in the Caribbean Sea in a terrible storm, had to run them ashore on the Island of Jamaica—where, laid up for a long and miserable year—1503—he was taken very sick, had several relapses, his men revolted, and death seem'd daily imminent; though he was eventually rescued, and sent home to Spain to die, unrecognized, neglected and in want. . . . It is only ask'd, as preparation and atmosphere for the following lines, that the bare authentic facts be recall'd and realized, and nothing contributed by the fancy. See, the Antillean Island, with its florid skies and rich foliage and scenery, the waves beating the solitary sands, and the hulls of the ships in the distance. See, the figure of the great Admiral, walking the beach, as a stage, in this sublimest tragedy—

for what tragedy, what poem, so piteous and majestic as the real scene?—and hear him uttering—as his mystical and religious soul surely utter'd, the ideas following—perhaps, in their equivalents, the very words.[2]

The headnote contains such vivid instructions to the reader on how to recreate imaginatively the setting for the poem that we might well conclude that Whitman made a mistake in dropping it.

The former titles of "The Sleepers"—"Night Poem" (1856) and "Sleep-Chasings" (1860)—are suggestive of Whitman's technique in this remarkable poem. Beginning with the opening line, "I wander all night in my vision," the poet portrays himself and his world of dreams and half-dreams as he lingers at first on the edges of sleep in Sections 1–2, then falls into deep sleep in Sections 3–6, then lingers once again in emerging from sleep on the edge of waking in Sections 7–8. The poem is in many ways a dramatization of that hypnogogic state, filled with its fantastic and hallucinatory images, out of which Edgar Allan Poe often constructed his stories and poems.

Near the opening of the poem, the poet characterizes the nature of his "sleep-chasings": "Wandering and confused, lost to myself, ill-assorted, contradictory, / Pausing, gazing, bending, and stopping." At first he seems merely an observer, but one freed from his ties to a particular place, randomly cataloging all he sees: "The wretched features of ennuyés, the white features of corpses, the livid faces of drunkards, the sick-gray faces of onanists." Then he begins to assume varied roles: "I dream in my dream all the dreams of the other dreamers, / And I become the other dreamers." Obscure and indeterminate sexual references increase and multiply, with the dreamer at one moment one of "a gay gang of blackguards! with mirth-shouting music and wild-flapping pennants of joy!" and at another moment a woman receiving in the dark her "truant lover," who addresses the night after his departure: "Darkness, you are gentler than my lover, his flesh was sweaty and panting, / I feel the hot moisture yet that he left me."

After the present Section 1, the following lines appeared and

remained in the poem until they were excluded from the 1881 edition.
Many critics believe that Whitman erred in excluding them, as they
are some of the most effective he wrote, and serve as an excellent
ending for the series of surrealistic images of Section 1:

> O hotcheek'd and blushing! O foolish hectic!
> O for pity's sake, no one must see me now! my clothes were stolen
>   while I was abed,
> Now I am thrust forth, where shall I run?
>
> Pier that I saw dimly last night when I looked from the windows!
> Pier out from the main, let me catch myself with you and stay—I will
>   not chafe you;
> I feel ashamed to go naked about the world,
> And am curious to know where my feet stand—and what is this
>   flooding me, childhood or manhood—and the hunger that crosses
>   the bridge between.
>
> The cloth laps a first sweet eating and drinking,
> Laps life-swelling yolks—laps ear of rose-corn, milky and just
>   ripened;
> The white teeth stay, and the boss-tooth advances in darkness,
> And liquor is spilled on lips and bosoms by touching glasses, and the
>   best liquor afterward.[3]

This deleted passage begins with a common dream experience, of
suddenly appearing naked and exposed in the world of the clothed,
and feeling the frantic need to hide oneself out of shame. The poet's
nakedness is, in the passage, prologue to what appears to be some
kind of sexual experience, which is transferred through dream from
the bedroom to a pier on the ocean (a place always sexually charged
for Whitman). The experience appears to have many of the elements
of a wet dream, especially in view of the distorted sexual images into
which the experience is translated in the closing lines—the lapping
cloth, the "life-swelling yolks," the "ear of rose-corn, milky and just
ripened," and others.

Whereas the first two sections of "The Sleepers" seem to move erratically and swiftly from one to another fragmentary and often opaque image, the central four sections of the poem present sustained scenes, clear and comprehensible. Yet the world is still the nighttime world of the sleepers, and the scenes represent the dreams of the poet. Section 3 portrays the poet as he watches a "gigantic swimmer swimming naked" but losing the struggle to reach the shore, his body first washed up to shore and then borne away by the violent waves. In Section 4, the poet first observes in the night a ship wrecked at sea, and then, the next morning, joins the crowd on the beach picking up the dead. In Section 5, the poet observes two moving revolutionary war scenes, the first of General George Washington and his troops suffering a defeat in the Battle of Brooklyn Heights (1776), the second of General Washington bidding goodbye to his troops after peace is declared in 1781 ("The chief encircles their necks with his arm and kisses them on the cheek").

In Section 6, the poet retells the story his mother had told him of the time "when she was a nearly grown girl living home with her parents on the old homestead." A "red squaw" had appeared at the door, looking for work, and the poet's mother had looked on her in "delight and amazement":

> The more she look'd upon her she loved her,
> Never before had she seen such wonderful beauty and purity,
> She made her sit on a bench by the jamb of the fireplace, she cook'd
> food for her,
> She had no work to give her, but she gave her remembrance and
> fondness.

After the Indian woman's departure, the poet's mother thought of her and watched for her and longed for her: "But the red squaw never came nor was heard of there again."

The meaning of these vignettes in Sections 3–6 is obscure, and, granting their nature as dreams, no doubt symbolic. Sections 3 and 4 contain scenes of ocean and death, Sections 5 and 6 scenes of land and love. Their juxtaposition—ocean and land, death and love—suggests subterranean or symbolic connections. The love portrayed in Section 5, Washington's love for his soldiers, and in Section 6, the mother's love for the red squaw, are instances of the kind of love explored in the "Calamus" poems. In the world of dreams, images merge and divide, fade and return, and may never yield their ultimate meanings. They contribute to that mystery which seems a permanent part of the experience of being and living.

In Sections 7 and 8, the images become again fragmentary and flowing, as in Sections 1 and 2. The poet seems to be emerging from his deep sleep, hanging on to the edge of waking. In Section 7, after presenting a catalog that seems to gather up many of the images that have appeared in the preceding sections—the "beautiful lost swimmer, the ennuyé, the onanist," the "laugher and weeper, the dancer, the midnight widow, the red squaw," the "consumptive, the erysipalite, the idiot, he that is wrong'd"—the poet exclaims:

> I swear they are averaged now—one is no better than the other,
> The night and sleep have liken'd them and restored them.

> I swear they are all beautiful,
> Every one that sleeps is beautiful, every thing in the dim light is
>   beautiful,
> The wildest and bloodiest is over, and all is peace.

Section 8 opens: "The sleepers are very beautiful as they lie un-clothed, / They flow hand in hand over the whole earth from east to west as they lie unclothed." There follows another catalog of the sleepers transfigured by night and sleep, joined to the flow of a spiritual and calming love:

> The bare arm of the girl crosses the bare breast of her lover, they
>   press close without lust, his lips press her neck,
> The father holds his grown or ungrown son in his arms with
>   measureless love, and the son holds the father in his arms with
>   measureless love,

> The white hair of the mother shines on the white wrist of the
>   daughter,
> The breath of the boy goes with the breath of the man, friend is
>   inarm'd by friend.

The leveling of night and the communion of sleep seem to become
metaphors for the leveling of death and the communion of the spiritual
world.

At the end of the poem, the sleepers "pass the invigoration of the
night and the chemistry of the night, and awake." The poet too wakes
to the day, but promises the night he will return. It is the night that
has shaped him, its dreams the source of much of his vital energy as
a poet:

> I love the rich running day, but I do not desert her in whom I lay so
>   long,
> I know not how I came of you and I know not where I go with you,
>   but I know I came well and shall go well.

> I will stop only a time with the night, and rise betimes,
> I will duly pass the day O my mother, and duly return to you.

The night is metaphorically the poet's mother, a return to the night a
return to the great womb of nature, sleep a symbolic representation
of and preparation for death, and death a kind of birth out of the
womb to spiritual life.

"To Think of Time" and "Whispers of Heavenly Death" complete
this third part of the *Leaves* and bring closure to its themes bridging
the way from life to death. The first of these seems to suffer a bit by
being placed next to "The Sleepers," one of the most remarkable
poems in the book. The conclusion of "To Think of Time" offers a
good example of its tendency to indulge in abstract exclamations:

I swear I think there is nothing but immortality!
That the exquisite scheme is for it, and the nebulous float is for it, and
   the cohering is for it!

And all preparation is for it—and identity is for it—and life and materials
are altogether for it!

"Whispers of Heavenly Death," a coherently shaped cluster of poems,
is considerably more successful, with a number of short poems that
sharply engage the reader's imagination: "Darest Thou Now O Soul,"
"Whispers of Heavenly Death," "Chanting the Square Deific," and
"A Noiseless Patient Spider."

Any attempt to get at Whitman's religious beliefs would need to
come to terms with "Chanting the Square Deific," a poem that distills
the varied elements of the religions of the world. By scandalously
including on equal terms the arch-rebel, the poem enlarges the trinity
to the four sides of the "square deific": Jehovah as law (or time), the
Consolator as love, Satan as revolt, and Santa Spirita as the all-pervasive unifying figure. They each define their roles, speaking in their own
voices, with Santa Spirita left to the last:

Santa Spirita, breather, life,
Beyond the light, lighter than light,
Beyong the flames of hell, joyous, leaping easily above hell,
Beyond Paradise, perfumed solely with mine own perfume,
Including all life on earth, touching, including God, including Saviour
    and Satan,
Ethereal, pervading all, (for without me what were all? what were God?)

As Jehovah represents judgment, the Consolator love, and Satan defi-
ance and rebellion, so Santa Spirita completes the square: "Life of the
great round world, the sun and stars, and of man, I, the general soul, /
Here the square finishing, the solid, I the most solid, / Breathe my
breath also through these songs." The poet's poetry is infused with
the "breath" of all four mythic figures, and particularly with that of
the one who completes and unifies the whole, Santa Spirita.

But it is in such a short poem as "A Noiseless Patient Spider,"
with its vivid image of the spider sending out its filaments, "ever
unreeling them, ever tirelessly speeding them," used as a symbol for
the soul's ceaseless search for a "bridge" to the divine, that Whitman

is at his most ingenious in capturing the restless search for spiritual authentication and certainty:

> And you O my soul where you stand,
> Surrounded, detached, in measureless oceans of space,
> Ceaselessly musing, venturing, throwing, seeking the spheres to
>   connect them,
> Till the bridge you will need be form'd, till the ductile anchor hold,
> Till the gossamer thread you fling catch somewhere, O my soul.

Whatever assurance the poet expresses so confidently elsewhere, this image of the soul endlessly seeking to connect, with the means of the connection a "gossamer thread," suggests such an uncertainty and fragility in the spiritual quest as to place the whole enterprise in precarious balance.

10

Night, Sleep, Death, and the Stars

In a section at the end of *Leaves of Grass* that parallels the opening section greeting the reader and announcing themes, Whitman concludes his book with poems that present a final review of his themes, in the process providing some guesses about the future and bidding farewell to the reader. Then, after the finished structure, Whitman adds his old age poems as Annexes. The relevant titles are: "Thou Mother with Thy Equal Brood," "From Noon to Starry Night," "Songs of Parting," and, as Annexes, "Sands at Seventy," "Good-Bye My Fancy," and "Old Age Echoes." As we might expect, there is an air of closure about all these works, something like a visit with old and familiar friends before a final parting. There is, moreover, nothing comparable in these poems and clusters to equal the Whitman masterpieces we have been examining. But there is a great deal of poetry of a very high order.

The opening lines of "Thou Mother with Thy Equal Brood," presenting a vision of the future of the Union preserved by the Civil War, set the tone:

Thou Mother with thy equal brood,
Thou varied chain of different States, yet one identity only,

Night, Sleep, Death, and the Stars

A special song before I go I'd sing o'er all the rest,
For thee, the future.

I'd sow a seed for thee of endless Nationality,
I'd fashion thy ensemble including body and soul,
I'd show away ahead thy real Union, and how it may be accomplish'd.

This poem is Whitman's final attempt to convey his political ideal as embodied in the democracy of the United States, the final in a series of poems stretching from "Starting from Paumanok" and extending through "By Blue Ontario's Shore."

Perhaps the most vivid image in "Thou Mother with Thy Equal Brood" is introduced in Section 2:

> As a strong bird on pinions free,
> Joyous, the amplest spaces heavenward cleaving,
> Such be the thought I'd think of thee America,
> Such be the recitative I'd bring for thee.

The bird (surely we are meant to imagine an eagle) is a metaphor for the Union, the brood (of the title) a metaphor for the states now bonded permanently after the Civil War. The bird's soaring "heavenward" is emblematic of its moving toward the democratic ideal, fully spiritualized:

Thou! mounting higher, diving deeper than we knew, thou
    transcendental Union!
By thee fact to be justified, blended with thought,
Thought of man justified, blended with God,
Through thy idea, lo, the immortal reality!
Through thy reality, lo, the immortal idea!

Unfortunately, Whitman's rhetoric tends to outsoar his craft in "Thou Mother," as in this parenthetical passage in Section 6: "(Lo, where arise three peerless stars, / To be thy natal stars my country, Ensemble, Evolution, Freedom, / Set in the sky of Law.)" We might well give our assent to the idea in these lines without feeling any freshness of imaginative conception in the way the idea has been embodied. Nevertheless the poem is important in rounding out Whitman's view of the Union's destiny.

"Thou Orb Aloft Full-Dazzling," the opening poem of the cluster "From Noon to Starry Night," is an invocation to a "hot October" sun addressed as a kind of celestial muse, with Whitman asking it to "strike through these chants"—help him to be creative in the autumn or afternoon of his career just as its "throes," "perturbations," "sudden breaks and shafts of flame gigantic" had inspired and infused his earlier poetry:

> Nor only launch thy subtle dazzle and thy strength for these,
> Prepare the later afternoon of me myself—prepare my
>   lengthening shadows,
> Prepare my starry nights.

"From Noon to Starry Night" ends with "A Clear Midnight" (a companion poem to "Thou Orb Aloft Full-Dazzling"):

> This is thy hour O Soul, thy free flight into the wordless,
> Away from books, away from art, the day erased, the lesson done,
> Thee fully forth emerging, silent, gazing, pondering the themes thou
>   lovest best,
> Night, sleep, death, and the stars.

As elsewhere in the clusters of *Leaves of Grass*, we find in "From Noon to Starry Night" not just the new work of the poet, but poems that have been selected from all periods of his career, chosen on the basis of theme rather than chronology. Because a review of themes is intended, there is naturally an emphasis on diversity rather than unity. A number of poems in this cluster are worthy of close attention, including "Faces" (1855), "The Mystic Trumpeter" (1872), "To a Locomotive in Winter" (1876), "O Magnet-South" (1860), and "Old War-Dreams" (1865–66).

Night, Sleep, Death, and the Stars

It may come as a surprise to find what looks like a pessimistic poem opening "Songs of Parting," the last cluster of *Leaves of Grass*. In "As the Time Draws Nigh," the poet confesses to an indefinable dread ("I know not what darkens me"), and contemplates his own death: "Perhaps soon some day or night while I am singing my voice will suddenly cease." As the poem closes, the poet seems to be trying, with some doubt or uncertainty, to shore up his courage: "O book, O chants! must all then amount to but this? / Must we barely arrive at this beginning of us?—and yet it is enough, O Soul; / O soul, we have positively appear'd—that is enough." The mood of this poem is so uncharacteristic of Whitman that we may indeed wonder whether the affirmation at the end is but bravado.

As with the previous cluster, the poems in "Songs of Parting" have been drawn from various periods of Whitman's career, selected apparently on the basis of variety of theme, but with an increasing emphasis on poems of closure and farewell, as many of the titles indicate: "Song at Sunset," "As at Thy Portals Also Death," "My Legacy," "As They Draw to a Close," "Joy, Shipmate, Joy!" "Now Finalè to the Shore." It is noteworthy that we find among these poems a number devoted to the Civil War: "Ashes of Soldiers," "Pensive on Her Dead Gazing," and "Camps of Green."

But there can be little doubt that the greatest of the poems in this final cluster is that which ends it, "So Long!" In itself it is a review of Whitman's major themes, a call for fulfillment of the present's promise in the future, and a final goodbye. One line seems to summarize the three-part thematic structure of the *Leaves* we have been examining: "I have sung the body and the soul, war and peace have I sung, and the songs of life and death." At the end of "So Long!" Whitman returns to the other major character in *Leaves of Grass*, his companion the reader—You—in a passage of startling intimacy and effectiveness:

Camerado, this is no book,
Who touches this touches a man,
(Is it night? are we here together alone?)

It is I you hold and who holds you,
I spring from the pages into your arms—decease calls me forth.

O how your fingers drowse me,
Your breath falls around me like dew, your pulse lulls the tympans of
my ears,
I feel immerged from head to foot,
Delicious, enough.

Seldom have readers failed to feel the poet's presence when reading
these lines—precisely what he intended in what seems to be his final
love scene with You, his camerado.

Following this metaphoric moment of intense intimacy (after all
it is Whitman in the form of his book that the reader touches, and his
poetic energy that springs from the pages into the reader's arms), the
poet bids farewell to his constant (and ever shifting and changing)
camerado-reader:

Dear friend whoever you are take this kiss,
I give it especially to you, do not forget me,
I feel like one who has done work for the day to retire awhile,
I receive now again of my many translations, from my avataras ascending,
while others doubtless await me,
An unknown sphere more real than I dream'd, more direct, darts
awakening rays about me, *So long!*
Remember my words, I may again return,
I love you, I depart from materials,
I am as one disembodied, triumphant, dead.

Gone is the darkness of "As the Time Draws Nigh"; in its place is a
note of triumph, a suggestion of temporary parting. Although the
poem ends with "dead," the word has been redefined by the time we
reach it ("I may again return," "I depart from materials," "disembodied," "triumphant"). And even the title of this final song of parting,
"So Long!", is the informal American goodbye, with the implication
of "until the next time"; it is not suggestive of permanent separation.
The Annexes—"Sands at Seventy," "Good-Bye My Fancy," and

"Old Age Echoes"—have suffered neglect, overshadowed as they have been by the large structure of the basic *Leaves* that looms over them, and compared as they inevitably are with the large number of Whitman's masterpieces. The poems of the Annexes constitute an astonishing body of lyric poetry written in the final years of a poet of remarkable creative power, and deserve a better fate than they have had. They are characterized by a refreshing honesty and wry wit, as in "As I Sit Writing Here" (in "Sands at Seventy"):

As I sit writing here, sick and grown old,
Not my least burden is that dulness of the years, querilities,
Ungracious glooms, aches, lethargy, constipation, whimpering *ennui*,
May filter in my daily songs.

Ever the confessional poet, Whitman puts the very things in this poem that he says he hopes to keep out of his poetry! Readers should discover for themselves the poems they believe to be worthy of consideration, even overlooked masterpieces of lyric expression.

To conclude this latest journey of mine through the poems of *Leaves of Grass*, I turn to one of my favorites, the title poem of "Good-Bye My Fancy," which comes at the end of the second Annex. The closing lines of this poem, addressed intimately to the poet's "fancy," abruptly change direction. At first the poet believes that death will bring separation from his lifelong companion, his fancy; but upon reexamining this thought, he suddenly affirms his new-found belief that he and his fancy will remain one, even in death. The passage exhibits the humor, frankness, and determination running through these final poems and may stand by itself, as I think Whitman would have liked, to close this book (Who knows, dear reader, for all the distance, he may be looking at us now?):

Long have we lived, joy'd, caress'd together;
Delightful!—now separation—Good-bye my Fancy.

Yet let me not be too hasty,
Long indeed have we lived, slept, filter'd, become really blended into one;

Then if we die we die together, (yes, we'll remain one,)
If we go anywhere we'll go together to meet what happens,
May-be we'll be better off and blither, and learn something,
May-be it is yourself now really ushering me to the true songs, (who
    knows?)
May-be it is you the mortal knob really undoing, turning—so now
    finally,
Good-bye—and hail! my Fancy.

Notes and References

1. The Prolonged Birth Pangs of the Nation

1. "The Declaration of Independence," *An American Primer*, ed. Daniel J. Boorstin (New York: The New American Library, 1968), 86.

2. The woman suffrage movement began in the United States with the Seneca Falls Convention in New York State, 1848.

3. Walt Whitman, *Complete Poetry and Selected Prose* (Boston: Houghton Mifflin Co., 1959), ed. James E. Miller, Jr.; the edition contains the whole of *Leaves of Grass*, including the three Annexes and the rejected poems; and the prose includes the 1855 Preface to *Leaves of Grass*, the 1872 Preface to *As a Strong Bird on Pinions Free*, the 1876 Preface to *Two Rivulets* (vol. II of the Centennial Edition of *Leaves of Grass*), the 1888 Afterword, "A Backward Glance O'er Travel'd Roads," and the whole of *Democratic Vistas* (1871). Quotations from these prose items will hereafter be cited in the text. Quotations from the poetry are normally identified by poem title and section number, which enable readers to locate passages easily in any edition of *Leaves of Grass*; citations of *The Complete Poetry and Selected Prose* will be used only in cases where locating passages might prove difficult.

3. The Fight of a Book for the World

1. Ralph Waldo Emerson, "A Letter to Whitman," *Walt Whitman: The Measure of His Song*, ed. Jim Perlman, Ed Folson, and Dan Campion (Minneapolis: Holy Cow! Press, 1981), 1.

2. Walt Whitman, "Walt Whitman and His Poems," *The Poetry and Prose of Walt Whitman, with a Biographical Introduction and a Basic Selection of Early and Recent Critical Commentary*, ed. Louis Untermeyer (New York: Simon and Schuster, 1949), 531.

3. Walt Whitman, "To Emerson—August 1856," ibid., 521.

4. W. D. O'Connor, "The Good Gray Poet," *A Century of Whitman*

Criticism, ed. Edwin Haviland Miller (Bloomington: Indiana University Press, 1969), 23–24.

5. Published in *Putnam's Magazine*, January, 1868; reprinted in *Three Tales* (Boston, 1892).

6. See excerpt in *A Century of Whitman Criticism*, ed. Edwin H. Miller, 27–30.

7. William Michael Rossetti, "Walt Whitman's Poems," *The Poetry and Prose of Walt Whitman*, ed. Louis Untermeyer, 977–82.

8. See excerpt in *A Century of Whitman Criticism*, ed. Edwin H. Miller, 33–39.

9. Reprinted in *Walt Whitman: The Measure of His Song*, ed. Perlman et al., 5.

10. Algernon Swinburne, "Whitmania," *A Century of Whitman Criticism*, ed. Edwin H. Miller, 81–89.

11. Whitman's letter to Symonds is quoted and discussed in Gay Wilson Allen, *The Solitary Singer: A Critical Biography of Walt Whitman* (New York: Macmillan, 1955; reprinted Chicago: University of Chicago Press, 1985), 535–36.

12. See discussion of early works on Whitman, including Bucke's, in Gay Wilson Allen, *The New Walt Whitman Handbook* (New York: New York University Press, 1986), 2–9.

13. See Bucke on Whitman excerpted in *A Century of Whitman Criticism*, ed. Edwin H. Miller, 112–20.

14. Both essay and poem are reprinted in *Walt Whitman: The Measure of His Song*, ed. Perlman et al., 29–31.

15. T. S. Eliot, "Introduction," *Ezra Pound: Selected Poems* (London: Faber & Gwyer, 1928); reprinted in part in *Ezra Pound: A Critical Anthology*, ed. J. P. Sullivan (Baltimore: Penguin Books, 1970), 101–9.

16. See Gay Wilson Allen's "Walt Whitman and World Literature," Chapter V in his *New Walt Whitman Handbook*.

4. The Lyric-Epic Structure

1. *The Correspondence of Walt Whitman: Volume I, 1842–1867*, ed. Edwin Haviland Miller (New York: New York University Press, 1961), 246–47; hereafter cited in the text as *Corres*.

5. "Song of Myself": Tapping Primal Energies

1. Randall Jarrell, *Poetry and the Age* (New York: Vintage Books, 1959), 102–3.

Notes and References

6. The Omnisexual Vision of *Leaves*

1. Sigmund Freud, *Civilization and its Discontents*, trans. and ed. James Strachey (New York: W. W. Norton & Co., 1961), 48–50.

2. See Whitman's "Leaves of Grass: A Volume of Poems Just Published," *The Poetry and Prose of Walt Whitman*, ed. Louis Untermeyer, 538–41. A good treatment of Whitman and phrenology is Edward Hungerford, "Walt Whitman and His Chart of Bumps," *American Literature* 2 (1931): 350–84.

3. *The Complete Writings of Walt Whitman*, ed. Richard M. Bucke et al. (New York: G. P. Putnam's Sons, 1902), 9:150.

4. D. H. Lawrence, *The Symbolic Meaning: The Uncollected Versions of Studies in Classic American Literature*, ed. Armin Arnold (London: Centaur Press, 1962), 262–63.

5. An abridged version of Ann Gilchrist's "An Englishwoman's Estimate of Walt Whitman" appears in *A Century of Whitman Criticism*, ed. Edwin H. Miller, 33–39.

6. Kate Chopin, "A Respectable Woman," *The Awakening & Selected Stories*, ed. Barbara H. Solomon (New York: New American Library, 1976), 194–97. See Lewis Leary's treatment of the relationship between Whitman and Chopin in *Southern Excursions: Essays on Mark Twain and Others* (Baton Rouge: Louisiana State University Press, 1971), 169–74.

7. Wandering the Open Road

1. See *The Correspondence of Henry David Thoreau*, ed. Walter Harding and Carl Bode (New York: New York University Press, 1958), 442–45.

2. Ralph Waldo Emerson, "Nature," *Selections from Ralph Waldo Emerson*, ed. Stephen E. Whicher (Boston: Houghton Mifflin Co., 1957), 24.

8. The Real Parturition Years of America

1. See Walt Whitman, *Leaves of Grass: Comprehensive Reader's Edition*, ed. Harold W. Blodgett and Sculley Bradley (New York: New York University Press, 1965), 358.

9. Bridging the Way from Life to Death

1. See editors' note in *Leaves of Grass: Comprehensive Reader's Edition*, 420.

2. *Inclusive Edition: "Leaves of Grass" by Walt Whitman*, ed. Emory Holloway (New York: Doubleday & Company, 1926), 682.

3. Ibid., 683.

Selected Bibliography

Primary Works

Editions

Editions of *Leaves of Grass* appeared in 1855, 1856, 1860, 1867, 1871, and 1881; reprintings from existing plates were issued in 1876, 1889, and 1891–92 (see chapter 4). Editions recently reprinted and available include: Malcolm Cowley, ed., *Walt Whitman's "Leaves of Grass": The First (1855) Edition* (New York: Viking Press, 1959), and Roy Harvey Pearce, *"Leaves of Grass" by Walt Whitman: Facsimile Edition of the 1860 Text* (Ithaca, N. Y.: Cornell University Press, 1961).

Working editions of *Leaves*: Malcolm Cowley, ed., *The Complete Poetry and Prose of Walt Whitman*, 2 vols. (New York: Pellegrini & Cudahy, 1948); Emory Holloway, ed., *Inclusive Edition: "Leaves of Grass"* (New York: Doubleday & Co., 1926); James E. Miller, Jr., ed., *Walt Whitman: Complete Poetry and Selected Prose*, paperback (Boston: Houghton Mifflin, 1959); and Sculley Bradley and Harold W. Blodgett, eds,. *Walt Whitman: "Leaves of Grass"* (New York: W. W. Norton, 1973).

The Complete Writings of Walt Whitman. Edited by Richard M. Bucke, Thomas B. Harned, and Horace L. Traubel. 10 vols. New York: G. P. Putnam's Sons, 1902.

The Collected Writings of Walt Whitman. General Editors, Gay Wilson Allen and Sculley Bradley. New York University Press, 1963–.

The Correspondence. 6 vols. Edited by Edwin H. Miller. 1961–77.

Daybooks and Notebooks. 3 vols. Edited by William White. 1978.

The Early Poems and the Fiction. Edited by Thomas Brasher. 1963.

"Leaves of Grass": Comprehensive Reader's Edition. Edited by Harold Blodgett and Sculley Bradley. 1965.

"Leaves of Grass": A Textual Variorum of the Printed Poems. 3 vols. Edited by Sculley Bradley et al. 1980.

Notebooks and Unpublished Prose Manuscripts. 6 vols. Edited by Edward F. Grier, 1984.

Prose Works 1892. 2 vols. Edited by Floyd Stoval. 1963–64.

Manuscripts and Miscellaneous Writings

American Bard. by Walt Whitman: The Original Preface to "Leaves of Grass" Arranged in Verse. Arranged by William Everson. New York: Viking Press, 1982.

An American Primer. Edited by Horace Traubel. Boston: Small, Maynard & Co., 1904. Reissued with an afterword by Gay Wilson Allen. Stevens Point, Wis.: Holy Cow! Press, 1987.

Calamus. Edited by Richard Maurice Bucke. Boston: Laurens Maynard, 1897. Letters to Peter Doyle written 1868–80.

Civil War Letters of George Washington Whitman. Edited by Jerome Loving. Introduction by Gay Wilson Allen. Durham, N.C.: Duke University Press, 1975. Valuable primary materials.

Dear Brother Walt: Letters of Thomas Jefferson Whitman. Edited by Dennis Berthold and Kenneth Price. Kent, O.: Kent State University Press, 1985. Valuable primary source materials.

Faint Clews and Indirections: The Manuscripts of Walt Whitman and His Family. Edited by Clarence Cohdes and Rollo G. Silver. Durham, N.C.: Duke University Press, 1949.

The Gathering of the Forces. Edited by Cleveland Rodgers and John Black. 2 vols. New York: G. P. Putnam's Sons, 1920. Material from the Brooklyn *Daily Eagle*, 1846–47.

The Half-Breed and Other Stories. Edited by Thomas Ollive Mabbott. New York: Columbia University Press, 1927. Five short stories.

I Sit and Look Out. Edited by Emory Holloway and Vernolian Schwarz. New York: Columbia University Press, 1932. Editorials from the Brooklyn *Daily Times*, 1857–59.

In Re Walt Whitman. Edited by Horace L. Traubel, Richard Maurice Bucke, and Thomas B. Harned. Philadelphia: David McKay, 1893. A memorial volume containing tributes and some Whitman materials, such as the 1855 reviews.

The Letters of Anne Gilchrist and Walt Whitman. Edited by Thomas B. Harned. New York: Doubleday, Doran & Co., 1918. Letters of a love affair that never materialized.

New York Dissected. Edited by Emory Holloway and Ralph Adimari. New York: R. R. Wilson, 1936. Articles from *Life Illustrated*, 1855–56.

The Uncollected Poetry and Prose of Walt Whitman. Edited by Emory Holloway. 2 vols. Garden City, N.Y.: Doubleday, Page & Co., 1921. Early poems and prose, manuscripts, notebooks, and novel, *Franklin Evans. or The Inebriate.*

Walt Whitman and the Civil War. Edited by Charles I. Glicksberg. Philadelphia: University of Pennsylvania Press, 1933. A collection of articles and manuscripts.

Walt Whitman Looks at the Schools. Edited by Florence Bernstein Freedman. New York: King's Crown Press, 1950. Articles on education from the Brooklyn *Evening Star* and the Brooklyn *Daily Eagle.*

Walt Whitman of the New York "Aurora": Editor at Twenty-Two. Edited by Joseph Jay Rubin and Charles H. Brown. State College, Pa.: Bold Eagle Press, 1950. Articles from the New York *Aurora,* 1842.

Walt Whitman's Workshop. Edited by Clifton Joseph Furness. Cambridge: Harvard University Press, 1928. Notes for lectures and manuscripts for essays and introductions to the *Leaves.*

Whitman's Manuscripts: "Leaves of Grass" (1860). Edited by Fredson Bowers. Chicago: University of Chicago Press, 1955. Contains important manuscripts for the "Calamus" and other sections.

With Walt Whitman in Camden. Horace Traubel. Vol. 1: *March 28–July 14, 1888.* Boston: Small, Maynard & Co., 1906. Vol. 2: *July 16–October 31, 1888.* New York: Appleton & Co., 1908. Vol. 3: *November 1, 1888–January 20, 1889.* New York: Mitchell Kennerly, 1914. Vol. 4: *January 21–April 7, 1889.* Philadelphia: University of Pennsylvania Press, 1953. Vol. 5: *April 8–September 14, 1889.* Carbondale: Southern Illinois University Press, 1964. Vol. 6: *15 September 1889 to 6 July 1890.* Carbondale: Southern Illinois University Press, 1982. Vol. 7: *July 7, 1890–February 10, 1891,* Carbondale: Southern Illinois University Press, 1991. Invaluable source for Whitman's recorded conversations.

The Wound-Dresser. Edited by Richard Maurice Bucke. Boston: Small, Maynard & Co., 1898. Letters written from the hospitals in Washington, D.C., during the Civil War.

Secondary Works

Studies

Allen, Gay Wilson. *The New Walt Whitman Handbook.* New York: New York University Press, 1975 (updated 1986). Replaces *Walt Whitman Handbook* (Chicago: Packard & Company, 1946). Indispensable for the serious student of Whitman.

———. *A Reader's Guide to Walt Whitman*. New York: Farrar, Straus & Giroux, 1970. A good introduction.

———. *The Solitary Singer: A Critical Biography of Walt Whitman*. New York: Macmillan, 1955; rev. ed.: New York: New York University Press, 1967; reprinted with 1984 preface: Chicago: University of Chicago Press, 1985. The most detailed and probably the definitive biography.

———. *Walt Whitman, as Man, Poet, and Legend*. Carbondale: Southern Illinois University Press, 1961. Contains key essays on Whitman by long-time Whitman critic, Allen.

———. Editor. *Walt Whitman Abroad*. Syracuse, N.Y.: Syracuse University Press, 1955. Translations of criticism from Germany, France, Scandinavia, Russia, Italy, Spain and Latin America, Israel, Japan, and India.

Arvin, Newton. *Whitman*. New York: Macmillan, 1938. Stresses political and economic views of Whitman.

Aspiz, Harold. *Walt Whitman and the Body Beautiful*. Urbana: University of Illinois Press, 1980. Explores relation of Whitman's poetry to nineteenth-century pseudoscience.

Asselineau, Roger. *The Evolution of Walt Whitman: The Creation of a Personality*. Cambridge: The Belknap Press of Harvard University, 1960. *The Evolution of Walt Whitman: The Creation of a Book*. Cambridge: The Belknap Press of Harvard University, 1962. Originally published as *L'Evolution de Walt Whitman: Après la première édition des Feuilles d'herbe*. Paris: Didier, 1954. A useful and interesting treatment from the French perspective.

Bailey, John Cann. *Walt Whitman*. New York: Macmillan, 1926. A brief and general early treatment that is still useful.

Barrus, Clara. *Whitman and Burroughs, Comrades*. New York: Houghton Mifflin, 1931. Valuable as a source for many documents.

Barton, William Eleazar. *Abraham Lincoln and Walt Whitman*. Indianapolis: Bobbs-Merrill, 1928. Exhausts the possibilities on this interesting topic.

Bazalgette, Leon. *Walt Whitman, the Man and His Work*. Garden City, N.Y.: Doubleday, Page & Co., 1920. An early French view; still useful.

Beaver, Joseph. *Walt Whitman—Poet of Science*. New York: King's Crown Press, 1951. A valuable critical study.

Black, Stephen A. *Whitman's Journeys into Chaos: A Psychoanalytical Study of the Poetic Process*. Princeton, N.J.: Princeton University Press, 1975. Focuses on the poetry as a revelation of Whitman's emotional problems.

Blodgett, Harold. *Walt Whitman in England*. London: Oxford University Press, 1934. Comprehensive treatment of Whitman's reputation in England.

Bloom, Harold. "The Central Man: Emerson, Whitman, Wallace Stevens." In

The Ringers in the Tower. Chicago: University of Chicago Press, 1971. Useful in placing Whitman in relation to poets who come before and after him.

Briggs, Arthur E. *Walt Whitman: Thinker and Artist.* New York: Philosophical Library, 1952. Emphasizes Whitman's philosophy.

Broderick, John C. Editor. *Whitman the Poet.* Belmont, Calif.: Wadsworth, 1962. A useful collection of critical essays.

Bucke, R. M. *Cosmic Consciousness.* New York: E. P. Dutton & Co., 1901. A brilliant, erratic, perhaps wild—but provocative—study of Whitman and other mystics.

————.*Walt Whitman*, Philadelphia: David McKay, 1883. An early biography that Whitman helped to shape.

Byers, Thomas B. *What I Cannot Say: Self, Word, and World in Whitman, Stevens, and Merwin.* Urbana and Chicago: University of Illinois Press, 1989. Valuable exploration of Whitman's presence in two important later poets.

Cady, Edwin H., and Louis J. Budd. Editors. *On Whitman: The Best from "American Literature."* Durham, N.C.: Duke University Press, 1987. Valuable collection of useful commentary on Whitman's work.

Canby, Henry Seidel. *Walt Whitman, an American.* Boston: Houghton Mifflin, 1943. Stresses democratic element in Whitman.

Cavitch, David. *My Soul and I: The Inner Life of Walt Whitman.* Boston: Beacon Press, 1985. Provocative Freudian examination of the poetry in the context of family relationships.

Chari, V. K. *Walt Whitman in the Light of Vedantic Mysticism.* Lincoln: University of Nebraska Press, 1964. Authoritative reading of the poetry in the light of the mystical doctrines of the Upanishads of Hinduism.

Chase, Richard. *Walt Whitman Reconsidered.* New York: William Sloane Associates, 1955. An unusual and stimulating approach, particularly in its analysis of "Song of Myself" as a comic poem.

Cherkovski, Neeli. *Whitman's Wild Children.* Venice, Calif.: Lapis Press, 1988. Focuses on some 10 contemporary Whitmanians, including Allen Ginsberg, William Everson, Gregory Corso, and Lawrence Ferlinghetti.

Coyle, William. Editor. *The Poet and the President: Whitman's Lincoln Poems.* New York: Odyssey Press, 1962. Contains the poems and a large number of commentaries.

Crawley, Thomas Edward. *The Structure of "Leaves of Grass."* Austin: University of Texas Press, 1970. An attempt to find the structure of the whole of *Leaves of Grass.*

De Selincourt, Basil. *Walt Whitman: A Critical Study.* New York: Mitchell Kennerley, 1914. A pioneer critical study still of value.

Eby, Edwin Harold. *A Concordance of Walt Whitman's "Leaves of Grass" and Selected Prose Writings.* 5 vols. Seattle: University of Washington Press, 1949–54. An invaluable research aid.

Eitner, Walter H. *Walt Whitman's Western Jaunt.* Lawrence: University of Kansas Press, 1981. Useful biographical material.

Erkkila, Betsy. *Walt Whitman among the French.* Princeton: Princeton University Press, 1980. Important account of Whitman's influence in France.

———. *Whitman the Political Poet.* New York and Oxford: Oxford University Press, 1989. An informed and indispensable book for anyone interested in Whitman's attitude toward the political issues of his time; demonstrates that Whitman was indeed a "political poet" in the best sense of the term.

Faner, Robert D. *Walt Whitman and Opera.* Philadelphia: University of Pennsylvania Press, 1951; reprinted: Carbondale: Southern Illinois University Press, Arcturus Books, 1972. An excellent demonstration of how opera shaped Whitman's poetry.

Foerster, Norman. *American Criticism.* Boston: Houghton Mifflin, 1928. A review of the critical principles of major American writers, including Whitman.

Gardner, Thomas. *Discovering Ourselves in Whitman: The Contemporary American Long Poem.* Urbana and Chicago: University of Illinois Press, 1989. Valuable readings of long poems by John Berryman, Galway Kinnell, Theodore Roethke, Robert Duncan, John Ashbery, and James Merrill—all linked to Whitman.

Grosskurth, Phyllis. Editor. *The Memoirs of John Addington Symonds: The Secret Homosexual Life of a Leading Nineteenth-Century Man of Letters.* New York: Random House, 1984. Important background for the Symonds-Whitman correspondence.

Hindus, Milton. Editor. *Leaves of Grass One Hundred Years After.* Stanford, Calif.: Stanford University Press, 1955. Includes important essays by Hindus, William Carlos Williams, Richard Chase, Leslie Fiedler, Kenneth Burke, David Daiches, and John M. Murray.

Hollis, C. Carroll. *Language and Style in "Leaves of Grass."* Baton Rouge: Louisiana State University Press, 1983. Valuable application of linguistic and speech-act theory to the poetry.

Holloway, Emory. *Whitman: An Interpretation in Narrative.* New York: Alfred A. Knopf, 1926. A thoroughly informed study that remains eminently readable.

———. *Free and Lonesome Heart: The Secret of Walt Whitman.* New York: Vantage Press, 1960. Claims to have discovered the identity of Whitman's son.

Hutchinson, George B. *The Ecstatic Whitman: Literary Shamanism and the*

Crisis of the Union. Columbus: Ohio State University Press, 1986. Emphasizes Whitman as a priestlike shaman playing a public role.

Jaén, Didier Tisdel. *Homage to Walt Whitman: A Collection of Poems in Spanish, with English Translations and Notes.* English foreword by Jorge Luis Borges. University: University of Alabama Press, 1969. Invaluable collection, revealing Whitman's impact especially in Latin America.

Jarrell, Randall. "Some Lines from Whitman." In *Poetry and the Age.* New York: Alfred A. Knopf, 1953. An important, perceptive criticism by a poet.

Johnson, Maurice O. *Walt Whitman as a Critic of Literature.* Lincoln: University of Nebraska Press, 1938. Summarizes Whitman's critical opinions.

Kaplan, Justin. *Walt Whitman: A Life.* New York: Simon & Schuster, 1980. Popular, readable biography.

Kennedy, William Sloane. *The Fight of a Book for the World.* West Yarmouth, Mass.: Stonecroft Press, 1926. An early handbook of historical interest.

Killingsworth, M. Jimmie. *Whitman's Poetry of the Body: Sexuality, Politics, and the Text.* Chapel Hill: University of North Carolina Press, 1989. A useful examination and tracking of the sexuality in Whitman's poems, highlighting Whitman's growing conservatism as he grew older.

Krieg, Joann P. Editor. *Walt Whitman: Here and Now.* Westport, Conn.: Greenwood Press, 1985. Collects important essays delivered at a 125th-anniversary conference on *Leaves of Grass.*

Kuebrich, David. *Minor Prophecy: Walt Whitman's New American Religion.* Bloomington: Indiana University Press, 1989. An astute and persuasive reexamination of Whitman as a religious prophet.

Larson, Kerry C. *Whitman's Drama of Consensus.* Chicago and London: The University of Chicago Press, 1988. A close and detailed examination of the "dynamics" of Whitman's poetry, including meanings hovering above and beneath the lines.

Lawrence, D. H. *Studies in Classic American Literature.* New York: Albert Boni, 1923. Offbeat, daring, and brilliant.

Lewis, R. W. B. Editor. *The Presence of Walt Whitman.* New York: Columbia University Press, 1962. Treats both the direct and indirect influence of Whitman on successor poets.

Loving, Jerome. *Emerson, Whitman and the American Muse.* Chapel Hill: University of North Carolina Press, 1982. Excellent exploration of the Emerson-Whitman relationship.

Marki, Ivan. *The Trial of the Poet: An Interpretation of the First Edition of "Leaves of Grass."* New York: Columbia University Press, 1976. A defense of the first edition as the best.

Masters, Edgar Lee. *Whitman.* New York: Charles Scribner's Sons, 1937. A pedestrian but competent biography.

Matthiessen, Francis Otto. *American Renaissance*. New York: Oxford University Press, 1941. A pioneer study of America's mid-nineteenth-century writers, including Whitman.

Mendelson, Maurice. *Life and Work of Walt Whitman: A Soviet View*. Moscow: Progress Publishers, 1976. Important account of Whitman's impact in Russia.

Middlebrook, Diane Wood. *Walt Whitman and Wallace Stevens*. Ithaca, N.Y.: Cornell University Press, 1974. Valuable exploration of the connections between two poets so apparently different.

Miller, Edwin H. *Walt Whitman's Poetry: A Psychological Journey*. New York: New York University Press, 1968. A tactful psychoanalytical reading that respects the poetry.

———. *Walt Whitman's "Song of Myself": A Mosaic of Interpretations*. Iowa City: University of Iowa Press, 1989. A very useful collation of and guide to the various interpretations of "Song of Myself."

———. Editor. *A Century of Whitman Criticism*. Bloomington: University of Indiana Press, 1969. Excellent and useful collection.

Miller, James E., Jr. *The American Quest for a Supreme Fiction: Whitman's Legacy in the Personal Epic*. Chicago: University of Chicago Press, 1979. Account of successor poets (Pound, Eliot, Crane, Williams, Berryman, and others) who took over Whitman's innovative form—the personal epic.

———. *A Critical Guide to "Leaves of Grass."* Chicago: University of Chicago Press, 1957. Critical analyses of the important poems and of the structure of the *Leaves* as a whole.

———. *Walt Whitman*. Boston: Twayne Publishers, 1962; updated ed., 1990. A useful, concise overview of Whitman's life and work.

———. "Walt Whitman's Omnisexual Vision," *The Chief Glory of Every People*, ed. Mathew J. Bruccoli (Carbondale: Southern Illinois University Press, 1973). Makes the case for portrayal of a complex and comprehensive human sexuality in Whitman's poetry.

———. "Whitman's *Leaves* and the American 'Lyric Epic,' " *Poems in Their Place* ed. Neil Fraistat (Chapel Hill: University of North Carolina Press, 1986). Explores the influence of Whitman's original poetic form on later American poets.

Miller, James E., Jr., Bernice Slote, and Karl Shapiro. *Start with the Sun*. Lincoln: University of Nebraska Press, 1960. A study of the Whitman tradition with emphasis on Hart Crane, D. H. Lawrence, and Dylan Thomas.

Moss, Howard. "A Candidate for the Future." *New Yorker*, 14 September 1981. An excellent review essay emphasizing Whitman's historical importance.

Selected Bibliography

Musgrove, S. *T. S. Eliot and Walt Whitman*. Wellington: New Zealand University Press, 1952. A persuasive argument that the relationship between the poets is deeper than usually believed.

Noyes, Carleton Eldredge. *An Approach to Walt Whitman*. New York: Houghton Mifflin, 1910. An enthusiastic early appraisal.

Pearce, Roy Harvey. Editor. *Whitman: A Collection of Critical Essays*. Englewood Cliffs, N.J.: Prentice-Hall, 1962. Emphasizes new perspectives on the poet.

Perlman, Jim, Ed Folsom, and Dan Campion. Editors. *Walt Whitman: The Measure of His Song*. Minneapolis: Holy Cow! Press, 1981. Invaluable collection of comments, prose and poetry, on Whitman by fellow poets and other writers.

Perry, Bliss. *Walt Whitman: His Life and Work*. New York: Houghton Mifflin, 1906. A perceptive, highly readable brief work.

Pound, Ezra. "What I Feel about Walt Whitman." In *Selected Prose: 1909–1965*. Edited by William Cookson. New York: New Directions Books, 1973. An extraordinary "love-hate" tribute.

Price, Kenneth M. *Whitman and Tradition: The Poet in His Century*. New Haven and London: Yale University Press, 1990. A valuable examination of the influences on Whitman; provides a rich historical context and also examines Whitman's influence on both novelists and poets of the premodernist period.

Santayana, George. "The Poetry of Barbarism." In *Interpretations of Poetry and Religion*. New York: Charles Scribner's Sons, 1900. Whitman's primitivism stressed.

Schyberg, Frederik. *Walt Whitman*. Translated by Evie Allison Allen. New York: Columbia University Press, 1951. Valuable detailed treatment of the various editions.

Sedgwick, Eve Kosofsky. "Coda: English Readers of Whitman." In *Between Men: English Literature and Male Homosexual Desire*. New York: Columbia University Press, 1985. An exploration of Whitman's psychosexual impact on British male readers.

Shephard, Esther. *Walt Whitman's Pose*. New York: Harcourt, Brace & Co., 1938. An eccentric but stimulating study of Whitman's "pose."

Shively, Charley. Editor. *Calamus Lovers: Walt Whitman's Working-Class Camerados*. San Francisco: Gay Sunshine Press, 1987. Focuses on the homosexual appeal in the "Calamus" cluster of poems.

———. Editor. *Drum Beats: Walt Whitman's Civil War Boy Lovers*. San Francisco: Gay Sunshine Press, 1989. Includes letters to Whitman from his soldier friends together with analyses of language that might (or might not) indicate actual homosexual relationships.

Stovall, Floyd. *The Foreground of "Leaves of Grass."* Charlottesville: University of Virginia Press, 1974. An important historical-biographical study.

Symonds, John Addington. *Walt Whitman: A Study*. London: John C. Nimms, 1893. A personal testimonial valuable as sensitive, impressionistic criticism.

Thomas, M. Wynn. *The Lunar Light of Whitman's Poetry*. Cambridge: Harvard University Press, 1987. A reading of Whitman's poems (including some usually neglected) in illuminating historical context.

Walker, Jeffrey. *Bardic Ethos and the American Epic Poem: Whitman, Pound, Crane, Williams, Olson*. Baton Rouge and London: Louisiana State University Press, 1989. A useful study of the five poets as in the epic tradition initiated by Whitman.

Waskow, Howard. *Whitman: Explorations in Form*. Chicago: University of Chicago Press, 1966. Close reading of individual poems as discrete examples of particular forms.

White, William. *1980: "Leaves of Grass" at 125: Eight Essays*. Detroit: Wayne State University Press, 1980. A variety of essays, some quite valuable.

———. Editor. *The Bicentennial of Walt Whitman: Essays from the "Long-Islander."* Detroit: Wayne State University Press, 1976. Various useful essays brought together.

White, William, and Ed Folsom. Editors. *Walt Whitman Quarterly Review*. Iowa City: Department of English, University of Iowa. Appears four times a year.

Willard, Charles B. *Whitman's American Fame*. Providence, R.I.: Brown University Press, 1950. Excellent reference work tracing Whitman's reputation after his death in 1892.

Woodress, James. Editor. *Critical Essays on Walt Whitman*. Boston: G. K. Hall, 1983. Useful collection of pieces by Whitman critics and scholars.

Zweig, Paul. *Walt Whitman: The Making of the Poet*. New York: Basic Books, 1984. A highly readable and sensitive biography by a poet.

Bibliographies

Allen, Evie Allison. "A Check List of Whitman Publications 1945–1960." In *Walt Whitman as Man, Poet, and Legend*, edited by Gay Wilson Allen. Carbondale: Southern Illinois University Press, 1961.

Allen, Gay Wilson. *The New Walt Whitman Handbook*. New York: New York University Press, 1975 (updated 1986).

American Literary Scholarship: An Annual. Durham, N.C.: Duke University Press, 1963–. Includes a chapter devoted to Whitman.

Selected Bibliography

Asselineau, Roger. "Walt Whitman." In *Eight American Authors: Revised Edition*, edited by James Woodress. New York: W. W. Norton & Co., 1971.

Boswell, Jeanetta. *Walt Whitman and the Critics: A Checklist of Criticism, 1900–1978*. Metuchen, N.J.: Scarecrow Press, 1980.

Giantvalley, Scott. *Walt Whitman, 1838–1939: A Reference Guide*. Boston: G. K. Hall, 1981.

Kummings, Donald D. *Walt Whitman, 1940–1975: A Reference Guide*. Boston: G. K. Hall, 1982.

White, William, and Ed Folsom. Editors. *Walt Whitman Quarterly Review*. Iowa City: Department of English, University of Iowa. Appears four times a year and contains an annotated bibliography.

Index

131

Index

THE AUTHOR

James E. Miller, Jr., is the Helen A. Regenstein Professor of Literature Emeritus at the University of Chicago, where he began teaching in 1962. In 1957 he published *A Critical Guide to Leaves of Grass*, which won the Walt Whitman Award of the Poetry Society of America. In 1959 he edited *Walt Whitman: Complete Poetry and Selected Prose* and in 1960 co-authored *Start with the Sun*, a book on the Whitman tradition of cosmic poetry that won the Poetry Chap-Book Award of the Poetry Society of America. His first edition of *Walt Whitman*, in Twayne's United States Authors Series, appeared in 1962, and was updated in 1990. In 1979, he published *The American Quest for a Supreme Fiction: Whitman's Legacy in the Personal Epic*. Miller has also authored *Quests Surd and Absurd: Essays in American Literature* (1967), *T. S. Eliot's Personal Waste Land: Exorcism of the Demons* (1977), and books on Herman Melville, F. Scott Fitzgerald, and J. D. Salinger.

Miller took his B. A. at the University of Oklahoma, and his M. A. and Ph. D. at the University of Chicago. He has taught at the University of Nebraska, where he served as chairman of the Department of English, a position he later held at the University of Chicago. He has held

Fulbright grants to lecture in Australia and to teach in Italy and Japan and has received two appointments to teach at the Sorbonne in Paris. He was appointed the Otto Salgo Professor of American Studies at the University of Budapest for the years 1991–92 and 1992–93. In 1970 he served as president of the National Council of Teachers of English, and in 1984 as president of the Association of Departments of English (of the Modern Language Association).